No. 2 in the Harnessing Health Information series

Series Editor
Michael Rigby

Using the Internet in Healthcare

Stuart Tyrrell

Radcliffe Medical Press

Radcliffe Medical Press
18 Marcham Road, Abingdon, Oxon OX14 1AA

British Library Cataloguing in Publication Data

A catalogue record for this book is available from the British Library.

ISBN 1 85775 366 6

Typeset by Joshua Associates Ltd, Oxford
Printed and bound by TJ International Ltd, Padstow, Cornwall

Contents

Series Editor's Preface

Using the Internet in Healthcare

The Internet is typical of so many aspects of the new information technology phenomenon – simultaneously both exciting and frightening, enabling yet threatening. We know of its power and potential, yet few admit to really understanding it. Within healthcare, many know of the wealth of health material it contains, yet there is also uncertainty as to the reliability of the material contained, and concern as to safety and security.

Given its rapidly growing role, a sound basic understanding of the Internet is essential for health staff when harnessing health information to support and enrich their daily practice. As with other health technologies a full scientific understanding is not necessary, but an appreciation of key features is a must. Unfortunately, the general reader has previously had little choice between technically dominated texts, and those which take rapid runs through a range of 'interesting' sites, many of which will change.

Stuart Tyrrell has now filled this gap, with *Using the Internet in Healthcare*. This has been given a high priority in the *Harnessing Health Information* series because of the Internet's importance as a widely available information resource, but one needing due diligence.

Information users in healthcare, whether clinician, manager or information staff, will find their needs well met by Stuart's easily readable, informative, but fact-packed text. He ensures understanding by starting with a clear explanation of the origins of the Internet and its workings, then goes on to describe how to harness its most common usage – E-mail. He then spends several chapters systematically explaining the World Wide Web, its various characteristics and services, and how to make full and effective use of it. This leads on naturally to discussion of Intranets, and an NHS case study by Mike Ingham. The book continues with a beginner's guide to web site design, then how to identify existing useful sites, and concludes with a realistic look at the future.

The Internet is clearly here to stay. To the informed health worker, its sound use is an essential part of *Harnessing Health Information*. I hope you will enjoy reading it and, as a result, become confident and competent in *Using the Internet in Healthcare*.

Michael Rigby
June 1999

About the authors

Stuart Tyrrell HND, DipHRM is Network Manager at the School of Postgraduate Studies in Medical and Health Care, Swansea. He obtained his HND in Business Information Technology at Bourne-mouth University, with a particular emphasis on applying Information Technology to the development of computerised solutions to business problems. He subsequently studied Human Resource Management at Luton University, gaining his postgraduate diploma.

He entered the health sector in primary medical care, developing and improving existing computerised information systems and then introducing new computer-based solutions. Subsequently he moved to the School of Postgraduate Studies in a technical support capacity in a busy department which includes the development and support of an integrated clinical information system used in acute hospital departments, as well as a range of applications within the School itself.

Stuart has developed a special interest and expertise based upon the Internet. He has provided seminars on its use, and teaches this on the School's courses. He has developed the School's own Internet and Intranet presence, and now manages the web site design service which is offered to local NHS organisations.

Mike Ingham MSc, DipHSM has been Head of Information Management and Technology with Lincoln District Healthcare NHS Trust since its formation in 1994. The Trust provides a comprehensive range of community-based health services to the people of central Lincolnshire, and in 1997 was awarded the Charter Mark for excellence in service to the public.

Before joining the NHS, Mike was a purser in the merchant navy, and has subsequently gained extensive experience in health service management and healthcare IM&T in the acute, community and long-stay settings. He was one of the first candidates to complete the Advanced Professional Diploma in IM&T (Health), established by the Institute of Health and Care Development for the NHS Executive.

Mike is a visiting lecturer at the School of Postgraduate Medical Education at the University of Warwick, where he gained his MSc in Health Information Science. His special interests are performance monitoring and the development of Internet technology in health-care management.

1 History of the Internet

What is the Internet?

The Internet is a collection of computers that span the globe and can be accessed by anyone with a computer and a modem. What differentiates the Internet from the computer networks found in most organisations is that the computers on the Internet are **Inter**-**net**worked. This means that instead of computer A linking to computer B and computer B connecting to C, computers on the Internet are inter-linked – so computer A is connected to both B and C. This gives the Internet its robustness, because if one computer fails, the connection will re-route itself around the failure.

Although the above is the correct definition of the Internet, the majority of users are not concerned with the structure of the Internet but consider the information stored on the inter-networked computers as the real Internet. The content of these computers varies from useful, well-researched information and services to the banal and sometimes libellous proclamations of other Internet users. However, the common theme of all this information, regardless of quality, is that it has been put onto the Internet to be shared with the global Internet user community for reasons that range from benevolent and commercial to misleading and inappropriate. And this is probably a better definition of the Internet, as it is a global information resource created and maintained by the Internet community for the dissemination of information.

Several methods are used to disseminate this information via the Internet, each offering slightly different methods of delivering information. The two main methods or 'protocols' that dominate the Internet today are E-mail and the World Wide Web. Other protocols include newsgroups, file transfer protocol, Archie, and chat. Both E-mail and the World Wide Web (also known as the Web or WWW) will be covered extensively in the course of this book, while the other protocols are covered in Chapter 7.

The origins of the Internet

The Internet can trace its roots back to 1969, when the US Department of Defense's Advanced Research Projects Agency developed, in conjunction with four universities, a fault-tolerant network that could survive a nuclear strike. The four original universities were the University of California at Los Angeles (UCLA), University of California Santa Barbara (UCSB), University of Utah, and Stanford University. This system, called ARPANET, was an inter-network of computers that allowed messages between two computers to travel over the network by a variety of routes. Therefore if one connection became inoperative, messages would still be able to travel between computers over the remaining communication routes. This was in stark contrast to the normal method of networking, where communications between computers travel over a defined route, and any fault in the path makes the communication link inoperative.

This feature gives the Internet great stability and robustness, as the network re-routes communications around any problems. For example, if one of the links between Europe and the USA were to fail, communication would be re-routed over another link. To the Internet user in the UK the only noticeable effect would be a possible reduction in speed when communicating with a computer in the USA.

The spread of the Internet

From its origins in the ARPANET the Internet has grown from the original four US computers to thousands scattered across the globe. This has happened through other computer system's administrators realising that a connection could benefit their organisation's exchange of information. As more organisations joined, the benefits became apparent to other sites and the number of connected computer systems snowballed. Therefore the Internet has grown organically, by spreading roots and branches into various types of organisations and institutions, rather than through an organised and predetermined strategy. The roots of the Internet are still within the research and education communities, and this means that it retains the ethos of freedom and easy exchange of information, and this pattern of organic growth is the source of many of the Internet's strengths and its weaknesses. One of the benefits of this organic growth is that the structure of the Internet is owned by a wide variety of organisations, providing a very competitive market for Internet services.

The leap from these communities into the mainstream has only really occurred in the 1990s, resulting in a system that is easy to use, even for a computer novice, based less on research and education, and more commercially orientated. The major driving force behind this change is the World Wide Web, an Internet protocol that makes the navigation of information stored upon the Internet intuitive and entertaining.

There are frequent reports in the media regarding the size of the Internet and predictions for the growth that it will experience beyond 2000. However, it is impossible to assess accurately the user base of the Internet as the unstructured format makes it impossible to measure accurately the number of connections at any given moment. In many ways these figures are irrelevant as an Internet connection is quickly becoming as ubiquitous as a telephone line, with anyone working for a large organisation expected to be available via the Internet.

What we can say confidently is that the Internet is a global resource, with almost every country in the world having some level of connection. The demographics show that the user base is concentrated in the USA, western Europe, and the Pacific Rim. The USA still dominates the Internet, both at work and at home, with western Europe rapidly catching up. The English language is also dominant, although the spread of other languages is quite visible, especially on the Web. An indicator of this is the translation service now offered by Alta Vista, one of the major search engines. The Graphics, Visualisation and Usability Center (GVU) at Georgia Tech. in the USA has run a survey of web usage every 6 months since 1994 and this gives a good indication of how the demographics of the Web have changed. The survey results can be found at: *http://www.cc.gatech.edu/gvu/user surveys/*

Development of the World Wide Web

The World Wide Web is the baby of the Internet protocols as it was initially conceived in 1989 at CERN, a large European physics project. An English researcher, Tim Berners-Lee, first put forward the idea of linking the information gathered by different research groups by using 'hyperlinks' in the text of the research findings posted on the Internet. This was important to the physicists at CERN, as there were a number of research groups scattered throughout Europe all working on interrelated projects. This made it difficult to follow the development of research projects, as the various reports and data that formed the basis of the overall project were distributed over a number of locations. Because the CERN physicists were enthusiastic users of the Internet, the gathering of related research information was fairly rapid, but it was not intuitive or easy. The use of hyperlinks gave the physicists immediate access to related information, regardless of where it was located or who had created it.

Hyperlinks were not a new idea, and had been used by Apple Macintosh users in the form of HyperCard for a number of years. The basic principle of hyperlinks is to allow the reader to follow the reference in a document to the original source of the quote. This creates links between related documents that allow the reader to jump from one document to another, regardless of whether the documents are stored on the same computer or on two computers on two different continents. The hyperlinks make the relating of information more intuitive and therefore easy for the reader to follow a path of related or interlinked documents.

TCP/IP

The heart of the Internet and the reason it is so robust is not solely the technology used to maintain the links between computer systems, but also the structure of the language used by the computers on the Internet. To enable communication between computers on a network, they must be talking the same language, or protocol, to allow each computer to understand the messages being transmitted and received. The protocol used by the Internet is called TCP/IP (transmission control protocol/Internet protocol). As the name suggests, this is not a single protocol but consists of two separate protocols – the transmission control protocol (TCP) and the Internetwork protocol (IP).

The principle features of IP are as follows.

- Every computer must have a unique address that identifies it on the Internet. This address (called the IP address) consists of four numbers, each of which ranges from 0 to 255, for example 125.16.87.224

- Any transmission between computers is broken down into small 'packets' that are sent individually over the Internet. It is more efficient to use a number of small packets rather than one large message.
- Each packet contains the IP address of the recipient and sender as well as the packet of information.

The transmission control protocol (TCP) is used to organise the packets sent using the Internet protocol, detailing the size of each packet, the total number of packets expected, and the order in which these packets should be arranged. It also checks the integrity of the packets and requests a re-transmittal from the sender if it receives a corrupted packet.

The aim of TCP/IP is to make communication over the Internet as efficient and as robust as possible. Using small packets of information rather than sending the message as a whole makes more efficient use of the available bandwidth, as a multitude of small packets can fit into a finite space more easily than a small number of large packets. Also, the autonomy of each packet, with each finding its own route between sender and recipient, gives any Internet communication a resilience not found in traditional computer networks.

One of the great advantages of the TCP/IP standard is that it is not limited to one software or hardware producer. Ever since the advantages of networked computers became available to the majority of organisations there has been a demand for an 'open' system which allowed a variety of computer hardware and software to communicate with one another. There have been a number of attempts at an open standard, but the majority have floundered due to the 'standard' being controlled by a small number of computer companies with their own agendas and interests. The Internet's lack of a controlling body has allowed TCP/IP to evolve into an open standard through the lack of commercial interests and resultant profit motives. This provides one of the most appealing features of the Internet, and its Intranet offshoot, as it allows users of a variety of computer systems to communicate seamlessly with one another.

Domain names

As mentioned, computers connected to the Internet can be identified by their unique IP addresses. However, IP addresses are not very memorable and contain nothing that can be used to identify the individual or organisation that uses the IP address. To make IP addresses more user-friendly, the numeric code of the IP address is ascribed to a more easily identifiable alphabetic code name called a 'domain name'. For example, the IP address 143.78.122.98 could be related to *somebody.somewhere.co.uk*

A domain name service (DNS) server that maintains a list of domain names and the corresponding IP addresses undertakes this task. This list is often referred to as a 'host table' as the IP address 'hosts' the domain name. The DNS service offers an additional benefit as, using this system, a Web site can be moved to another computer with a different IP address but still retain its domain name, and also one IP address can host a number of domain names. For example, *somebody.somewhere.co.uk* could be stored in the 'somebody' directory on the computer with the IP address 143.78.122.98 while *another.co.uk* could point to the 'another' directory on the same computer. This means that the number of domain names available is not limited by the finite combinations of 0 to 255 used by IP addresses.

The domain name is the unique address used to identify each computer on the Internet. Domain names are the electronic equivalent of postal addresses, allowing all Internet communications to find their target. For example, the *British Medical Journal* (*BMJ*) owns the domain name *bmj.com*

The domain name consists of two parts – the name of the organisation and the domain code (which may contain a country code).

In this example, the organisation's name is obvious, i.e. *bmj*. The importance of obtaining a domain name that is recognisable to your organisation is becoming increasingly recognised, especially for commercial organisations where on-line services could become an important source of revenue. This is illustrated by the case of Prince sportswear, a large American organisation, taking Prince, a small British computer company, to court over the right to use the domain name '*prince.com*' as they felt that it would be detrimental to their sportswear sales if they did not have the *prince.com* domain name.

There have also been numerous cases of people registering well-known names, such as Harrods, in an attempt to obtain large fees from the organisation that holds the trademark on that name — fortunately the courts have judged this illegal and this practice should disappear.

The domain code depends on the country in which the domain name is registered. There are two parts to this code, the first part denotes the type of organisation and the second the country in which the domain name is registered. However, the country code can be confusing as the US organisation codes do not have a related country code whereas others do.

This is made more confusing by the fact that an organisation does not have to register within the country in which it operates, and therefore does not always have the expected country code. Common country codes are shown in the table below. As mentioned above, the USA does not have a country code and, for this reason, is often referred to as the top-level domain.

Country Codes

Code	Description
.au	Australia
.ch	Switzerland
.de	Germany
.fn	France
.ie	Ireland
.jp	Japan
.uk	United Kingdom

The type of organisation is expressed by a code that reflects the origins of the Internet, with military, academic, government, and commercial organisations having equal billing. The organisation codes differ slightly between countries, and the table overleaf illustrates some common codes for UK domain names and also US (or top-level) domain names.

Organisational type codes

Code	Description
.ac	Academic organisation, e.g. university
.co	Commercial organisation
.com	Commercial organisation[*]
.edu	Educational organisation[*]
.gov	Government organisation[+]
.mil	Military organisation[*]
.net	Internet services organisation
.org	Non-commercial or non-profit-making organisation, e.g. research, institute[+*]

[*] Indicates a top-level domain organisational code.
[+] Indicates a top-level and regional organisational code.

These are some of the older codes available, however there are moves to introduce new codes to cover a wider range of organisations and to ease the demand for the above organisational codes.

As mentioned earlier, and illustrated in the *BMJ* example, an organisation does not have to register its domain name in the country in which it resides (i.e. the *BMJ* is not *bmj.co.uk*). The use of a top-level name has become increasingly common as it provides the organisation with a multinational stature at no extra cost. In this example the *BMJ* has chosen to use the top-level code for a commercial organisation (i.e. *com*).

The domain name forms the foundation of most Internet communication, but to connect with the computer represented by the domain name you need to also specify the Internet protocol used. Each protocol has its own standard additions to the domain name, the particular details for each protocol are detailed in the relevant sections later in this book. The details for the two most popular protocols, WWW and E-mail, are shown below.

- WWW – the address needs to be prefixed by *http://* to indicate that the hypertext transfer protocol is being used, and the domain name is normally preceded by www to indicate that you are connecting to the organisation's web site. For example, the *BMJ*'s web site would be *http://www.bmj.com*

- E-mail – as E-mails are sent to individuals rather than organisations, the domain name is preceded by the person name or user ID and the @ symbol. The syntax or ID used varies between organisations, and is normally administered within the organisation. For example if AN Other worked for the *BMJ*, their address could be *a.n.other@bmj.com*, or *another@bmj.com*, or even *sa4@bmj.com* if user IDs were used.

Bandwidth

The TCP/IP protocol is an efficient user of bandwidth, and one of the major concerns of any computer network is providing sufficient bandwidth for the amount of data being transmitted by the computers on the network. Bandwidth is the term used to describe the capacity of the cables that form the infrastructure of the network. It is normally measured in megabytes per second (Mbps) and this indicates the amount of data that can pass through the cable. The most common type of cabling used in local area networks (i.e. a network of computers on a single site, such as a hospital) has a bandwidth of 10 Mbps.

For the network manager, the two main worries regarding bandwidth are having enough to cope with the number of new users joining the network, and having enough to cope with the rising popularity of bandwidth-hungry multimedia applications. Both of these have seen massive growth on the Internet, with new users each year measured in millions and new World Wide Web multimedia applications appearing frequently.

Therefore, providing sufficient bandwidth to meet the needs of the rapidly expanding Internet community is a constant topic of conversation among Internet technophiles and managers. Many pessimists have predicted the collapse of the Internet based upon it running out of bandwidth and communications becoming jammed. The effects of a reduction in available bandwidth on the Internet can be seen every day as there is a noticeable reduction in performance after 11 a.m. in the UK, as American users start to come on line – increasing the amount of traffic on the Internet and the percentage of bandwidth used.

Connection is via third party

Hopefully, this book will help demonstrate to you the possible benefits that can be gained by accessing the Internet. But how do you actually connect to the Internet?

For most organisations the cost and time needed to maintain a permanent connection to the Internet is too great to be justified by the benefits accrued. This means that they use a third party called an Internet service provider (ISP) to maintain their link to the Internet. This can vary from an individual connecting indirectly via a modem, to the management of a large organisation's permanent connection and web site. This is explored further in Chapter 8.

Once a connection has been established, there is no additional charge for using most of the facilities available on the Internet. This also means that there is no difference in cost when accessing local or international Internet sites. There are a number of reasons for this, the primary one being that the Internet has evolved as an arena for free and open communication and this freedom is protected vigorously. The nature of the Internet would also make it very difficult to charge on a per-call or per-distance basis, as it is impossible to predict the exact route of a connection to a remote site. Each part of the communication finds its own route between the two parties, each taking a slightly different length of time to reach its destination. The diverse ownership of the Internet's infrastructure also mitigates against charging, as an Internet communication can travel through a wide variety of organisations' equipment before reaching its destination. Therefore it would be impractical to pay each individual organisation for carrying your transmission. These factors have helped the Internet expand as it allowed individuals and organisations to gain international connections at a fraction of the cost of other media.

Managing the infrastructure

The Internet is not controlled by any organisation, but there are a number of administrative bodies that help to maintain and develop the Internet. The closest to a central organisation is the Internet Architecture Board (IAB), which is a committee comprising Internet users who help to plan and implement any developments in Internet technology. For example, they have a pivotal role in the development of the next version of the Internet protocol (called IPng). This promises faster connections and an increase in the number of sustainable connections to the Internet in the future.

Other organisations undertake the administration of the various components of the Internet. Two that are of particular importance are the World Wide Web Consortium and the Internet Assigned Numbers Authority.

The World Wide Web Consortium (W3C) is an independent body that promotes and develops the standards used on the World Wide Web (WWW). It also holds details of the history of the WWW and demonstrates new developments in WWW standards. The W3C is a global organisation hosted by universities, funded by member organisations and headed by Tim Berners-Lee, the founder of the WWW. Its WWW address is: *www.w3.org*

Until recently, the Internet Assigned Numbers Authority (IANA) oversaw the distribution and development of domain names to registered organisations. It performed the pivotal role of maintaining the DNS system. The IANA was lead by Jon Postel, a researcher based at the University of Southern California, who had been involved with the Internet from its beginnings in the ARPANET. The Internet Corporation for Assigned Names and Numbers (ICANN) took over this role at the end of 1998, as the US government wanted to devolve their involvement in the organisation of the Internet. Perhaps the most important change is that ICANN is an international organisation (compare to the US-only IANA), reflecting the increasingly global nature of the Internet.

The important aspect of both these organisations is that they are non–profit-making organisations, with the primary aim of furthering the WWW and the Internet rather than financial gain. They perform pivotal roles within the infrastructure of the Internet from bases within academic organisations by setting standard, rather than forcing users to purchase their product.

The future of these philanthropic organisations and other issues are discussed further in Chapter 12, which looks at the future of the Internet

2 E-mail

Introduction

Electronic mail (E-mail) has established itself quickly as an invaluable communication medium alongside the telephone, fax, and traditional letter. It combines the formality and permanence of a written letter with the speed and immediacy of the telephone. E-mail offers the ability to communicate with people anywhere in the world for the price of a short local telephone call.

A common misconception regarding E-mail is the need to remain constantly attached to the Internet to ensure that messages are not missed. In reality, the time-consuming tasks of composing and reading E-mail are undertaken 'off line' (i.e. not connected to the Internet). You need only connect to the Internet to send out the messages you have written, and to collect any messages waiting for you, minimising the connection time as far as possible. When you are not connected, your E-mail messages are held on a computer (with a very large storage capacity) called a **mail server**. When you connect, your E-mail software automatically checks the mail server for any outstanding mail for your account.

The Internet protocol used for E-mail communication is known as SMTP (simple mail transfer protocol). This performs the basic functions of sending E-mail messages and converting any E-mail received into a readable format. However, it does not support the use of mail servers, so another protocol, called POP (Post Office protocol), performs this function. Modern E-mail packages use the third version of POP (called POP3) to receive and store incoming E-mail messages, while using SMTP to send E-mail. POP3 stores any messages addressed to you on the mail server, and when you connect you can choose whether to download these messages from the mail server onto your own computer. This also means that it is possible to access your E-mail messages from any computer connected to the Internet, as the messages are stored on a separate, remote computer until you download them.

Sending E-mail

When you create a new mail message you will be presented with a screen similar to that shown in Figure 2.1 (this is a screenshot of Microsoft's Outlook E-mail package). The structure of an E-mail message is based on the layout of a business letter, allowing you to enter the details of who the message is addressed to, who should receive copies, the subject matter, and finally the body text of the message. In addition, E-mail allows you to attach computer files containing text, graphics, sound, etc. to your message.

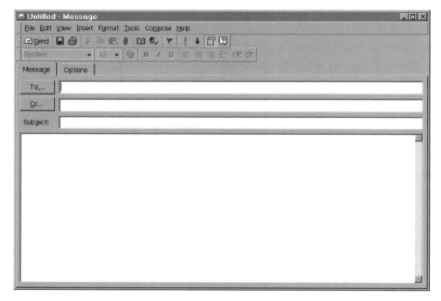

Figure 2.1 The structure of an E-mail.

The components of an E-mail message are:

To:

This is the address of the main recipient of the message. The body of the message should be aimed directly at this person (or persons).

CC:

The CC: stands for carbon copy, this is where you enter the addresses of anyone who should receive a copy of the correspondence. Some E-mail packages also offer a BC: section (for blind copy) which allows you to forward a copy of the E-mail to someone without their name appearing on the message received by the other recipients.

Subject:

The subject line allows you to give the message a heading for easy reference. The recipients will normally see only the subject of the E-mail and the address of the sender when they download the message from their mail server. Therefore, the subject of the message should be clearly relevant to the body of the message and pertinent to the recipients.

Message

This is where the actual body text of the message is entered. The 'netiquette' (the rules concerning communication via the Internet) of E-mail is discussed in greater depth later in this chapter, but some basic guidelines to writing E-mail messages are:

● there is no need to enter 'Dear . . .', etc. at the top of the message, as it is acceptable to forego this formality

● the recipient has to pay for the time taken to download the message, so make sure the message is brief and relevant.

Organising messages

There is a wide variety of E-mail packages available, ranging from basic shareware to groupware packages where E-mail is just one small component in a variety of workgroup communication tools. However, all packages follow the same basic structure for managing outgoing and incoming messages. The actual names given to the features detailed below may differ from package to package, but the basic function remains the same.

The out-tray

You can create an E-mail message within your E-mail package without connecting to the Internet. Once you have created your message you should be provided with the option of connecting to the Internet to send your message immediately, or to store the message in your out-tray. The out-tray acts as a repository for all unsent E-mail messages, storing the messages until a connection to the Internet is established. Once a connection is made, your E-mail package sends all pending messages from your out-tray in a concentrated, high-speed burst over the link. This keeps connection time to a minimum. Once a message has been sent, a copy of the message is retained – ensuring that you have a copy of the document for future reference.

The in-tray

The in-tray acts as a store for all messages retrieved from your mail server. When a connection to the Internet is made, the E-mail package performs a check for any mail messages waiting on the mail server, and downloads these E-mails into your in-tray. The messages in the in-tray can be read at your convenience, whether you are off-line or still connected, as they are kept on your computer. After reading, the messages can remain indefinitely in the in-tray, or be deleted after reading. To make storage and organisation of sent and received messages easier, your E-mail package provides a 'filing cabinet' for storing old messages.

Filing cabinet

The filing cabinet stores and arranges correspondence sent and received from your computer in a way that allows you to retrieve previous messages easily. It stores messages in chronological order and can also organise them into groups of related messages. Most packages will not automatically prompt you to move messages into the filing cabinet, but will leave them either in the out-tray or in-tray. However, after a short while you will find that the number of messages residing in your in and out trays will mount up, making it difficult to locate specific messages.

The address book

The filing cabinet organises your messages, but there is also a need to maintain the details of the E-mail addresses you use frequently. E-mail addresses need to be accurate, as there is no margin for error. The ability of a postal worker to discern incorrectly addressed mail and redirect it to the intended destination does not have an equivalent in the E-mail system. The case-sensitivity of E-mail addresses further compounds this requirement for accuracy, i.e. a capital 'H' is treated as a separate letter from a lower-case 'h'. Therefore, there is a need for the capability to store E-mail addresses that are used frequently, to prevent errors occurring when the address is re-typed each time that a message is sent. Thankfully, the address book is a ubiquitous feature of E-mail packages. The address book stores the E-mail address with the person's name to make it a more meaningful identifier than just the E-mail address, and you can normally also add comments or notes about the address. The addresses are then stored alphabetically with most packages also allowing you to organise further into groups of similar or related addresses. Addresses can be entered manually into the address book or can be extracted from received E-mails. Maintaining an address book does require some effort and discipline, but it can provide real benefits in the organisation of your E-mail communications.

Receiving E-mail

When you receive E-mail, it is stored in your in-tray until it is opened and read. Before reading, you can see only the E-mail address of the sender and the subject line of the message. On opening you will find the full text of the message, and, if there is an attachment with the message, an icon or symbol to indicate this.

You should also be presented with a number of options, covering the following:

- reply – automatically creates a message addressed to the sender, ready for your response to be added into the message part of the E-mail
- forward – sends a copy of the received E-mail to another address
- file – moves the message into the filing cabinet
- delete – permanently removes the message from your in-tray.

Attachments

One of the key advantages of E-mail over other communication media is the ability to 'attach' computer files to your E-mail messages. This allows you to send word-processed documents, spreadsheet workbooks, graphic images, etc. anywhere in the world from your computer. To attach a computer file to your E-mail message is simply a case of writing the message and then selecting the file on your computer to be sent with the E-mail message.

However, although attachments can provide quick and easy interchange of documents, they are a major cause of problems and frustrations. The two common difficulties are indecipherable or incompatible attachments and excessive file size.

A common cause of indecipherable attachments is where the sender sends a word-processed document as a text file instead of a binary file, in the misguided belief that because the document is text only (i.e. without graphics) it qualifies as text. The result of this error tends to be an attachment with a few pages of strange characters and symbols at the start and end of the document, with the text of the word-processed document, without formatting, sandwiched in the middle. An explanation of this is that different computer systems are capable of reading each other's E-mail as the messages are written in the lowest common denominator – ASCII (American standard code for information interchange) text, often referred to as plain text. However, attachments are rarely plain text documents – even simple word processor documents contain codes that are beyond the scope of ASCII text. This means that attachments need to be treated as binary format to preserve these codes, which is a problem to the E-mail system as it is designed to cope with only ASCII text. To overcome this, the binary attachment has to be converted to text in such a way as to enable it to be restored to its original binary format by the E-mail's recipient. The two main methods of performing this conversion are UUencoding (UNIX-to-UNIX encoding) and MIME (multipurpose Internet mail extensions). UUencoding is the older system and is now rarely used, as it requires the recipient to UUdecode the combined message and attachment upon receipt, whereas MIME attachments are automatically separated from the accompanying message by any MIME-compliant E-mail package. Nearly all E-mail packages sold now are MIME compliant – however, earlier versions may not be. It is advisable to ensure that your E-mail package is MIME compliant, especially if you will send or receive attachments regularly.

Another problem that often occurs is that the attachment is in a format, or produced in a software package, that is not compatible with any of the packages installed on the recipient's computer. This is further exacerbated by the ability of E-mail to be exchanged between computer systems with different operating systems or environments. The simplest solution to this problem is to ensure that the recipient does have a compatible software application installed on their computer, or to convert the file into a format that can be read by the recipient. Most software applications allow you to convert documents into earlier versions of the same application, or into a format compatible with their major competitors' software packages. Other options include converting word-processed documents into a standard format, such as Rich Text Format, and spreadsheet or database data into a simple standard, such as delimited text.

One of the major differences between E-mail and other communication media is that the majority of the cost, with regard to time and money, is borne by the recipient, as they must connect to the Internet and download your message. This should always be considered whenever you send circulars/advertisements or large attachments, as these are two possible sources of frustration and resentment.

As it costs the sender the same to send E-mail to 20 people as to one individual, it is obviously very tempting (and economical) to distribute widely the electronic version of junk-mail. However, the minor irritant of the traditional junk mail letter or flyer is worsened in the electronic equivalent by the fact that the recipient has had to pay to receive this message or advertisement. Therefore, it is understandable that most people have a low tolerance of junk E-mail, which is often referred to as 'spam', or of the perpetrators – called 'spammers'. Frequent or blatant spammers are often subjected to 'flaming', the term used to describe deliberate hampering of another user's Internet access in retribution for a breach in 'netiquette'.

Large attachments are an effective means of handicapping the E-mail system, whether it is done intentionally or in error. The effect of large attachments is becoming increasingly important as software packages produce documents of greater file size, combined with the increasing use of digital cameras and videos with their associated large image files.

Whenever you attach a file to an E-mail message, you should be aware of the size of the file. The most effective method of reducing file size is to use compression software, which can typically reduce the size of documents by 50 to 70%, although program files are unlikely to be compressed to this extent. The most common software of this type is a shareware package called PKZIP, which is widely available. Another, increasingly common, shareware package called WINZIP (*www.winzip.com*) gives the PKZIP compression program a friendlier, Windows-based interface.

E-mail on the NHS Intranet

E-mail is also a core component of the NHSNet, providing all the benefits of Internet E-mail to the health service. While the basic structure of E-mail on the NHSNet is the same as that used on the Internet, there are a few notable differences.

The first, and most noticeable, difference is that although there is a wide profusion of E-mail software packages available, users on the NHSNet are restricted to Lotus CC: Mail, Microsoft Exchange (with Outlook), or Novell GroupWise. These packages work in a slightly different manner to SMTP E-mail packages and use their own proprietary standards to provide their users with enhanced features unavailable to the ASCII text bound SMTP protocol. This does entail compatibility problems when communicating between the different packages, as each is optimised to work using its own standards and protocols. To overcome this, communication over the NHS Intranet adheres to the X.400 standard, as it provides more advanced and secure communication than that allowed by the SMTP standard, and provides a common communication standard for the different packages used within the NHS. However, if an E-mail message is sent to an Internet address from the Intranet, the message is converted into ASCII text and transferred to the recipient using SMTP. This conversion to a simpler format is not always flawless, and this is why some messages sent to Internet addresses can have minor formatting problems when read by the recipient.

Viruses

E-mail is an ideal method of disseminating information from computer to computer, unfortunately this also means it is an ideal method of spreading computer viruses. The threat of E-mail-borne viruses must be taken seriously by all organisations, as this has quickly become one of the most common methods of distribution.

Unfortunately, the real threat of virus infection from E-mail, and the resultant fear of infection, has led to a new type of virus – the hoax virus. The most notorious hoax virus is 'Good Times' which has spawned a number of variants and aliases. These hoaxes are very similar in format, warning of viruses that destroy the data on your hard disk automatically when the message is opened, and also being forwarded automatically to every address in your E-mail package's address book. The message ends by pleading with you to pass the warning on to anyone you know who uses E-mail. However, as E-mail messages consist only of ASCII text, it is impossible to spread viruses through the message or address part of the E-mail, only attachments are a possible source of infection. This means that it is not possible for a virus to automatically infect your PC directly from an E-mail message.

However, although the message cannot contain a virus, attachments are a prime source of infection. The advent of macro viruses, which are contained within documents (especially Microsoft Word) rather than being separate programs, has made it increasingly important to virus check any attached file received via E-mail. The major antivirus software vendors have recognised this and now offer software that is specifically geared to checking E-mail attachments.

Writing E-mail

As with any communication media, to make the most of E-mail you need to be aware of the etiquette of the medium (on the Internet this is referred to as 'netiquette') to ensure that your messages are not misunderstood or cause offence to other E-mail users.

Breaches in netiquette can result in punishment or 'flaming'. This entails the victims of the netiquette breach gaining revenge by attacking the perpetrator's E-mail system. This revenge can range from multiple E-mail responses, to the perpetrator's service provider being blocked out of the Internet.

There are many scare stories regarding new Internet users breaching 'netiquette' and being 'flamed' by the Internet community. However, because of the large increase in Internet usage and the vast number of new users joining each month, the rules have necessarily relaxed. The rules of netiquette are still relevant, and should still be adhered to as they are designed to help make the Internet run more smoothly for all users.

The rules outlined in this section are relevant to E-mail messages sent to individuals, or newsgroups (newsgroups are covered in more detail in Chapter 7). For newsgroup users, compliance with these rules is even more important as these tend to be more sensitive to breaches in netiquette and are notorious for flaming transgressors.

The first rule is to remember that the recipient has to pay to receive your message, so keep it brief and relevant and try to reduce the size of attachment as much as possible. The other rules are listed below.

- When writing your message there is no need to follow the layout of more conventional letters. It is acceptable to start the body text of the message immediately, without adding the recipient's address or a salutation at the beginning. If you do want to add a greeting at the start of the message, it is better to use something less formal than 'Dear. . .' such as 'Hello. . .' or just the person's name. This also applies to the end of the letter, where 'Yours sincerely . . .', etc. seems incongruous. Again if you do want to use a parting line, something more informal such as 'Thanks. . .' or 'Regards. . .' is appropriate. As it is impossible to sign E-mail in the same manner as a conventional letter, some users have created their own digital signatures. This normally takes the form of the person's name and E-mail address, with many adding a one-line quote or witticism to add personality. Most E-mail packages will allow you to add this automatically to the end of your message.

- As you cannot format E-mail text in the same manner as in a word processor (e.g. bold or underline text) it can be difficult to add emphasis to certain sections of the text. To get around this limitation, you can signify underlined text by placing a minus sign either side of the relevant passage, e.g. −this is underlined text−. Another method that can be used is to capitalise the text. However, too much capitalised text is regarded as shouting − which is a breach of netiquette (and is difficult to read).

- Because of the immediacy and informality of E-mail, it is often written in a brief, terse style. However, as the recipient has no vocal clues (as they would in a telephone call) to the mood of the writer, brief and terse can be misinterpreted as aggressive and unfriendly. To prevent this misunderstanding many E-mail writers use 'smilies' or 'emoticons' to convey moods. Some of the most commonly used (and some of the more bizarre) are shown in the table overleaf.

Symbol	Meaning
:)	Happy
:(	Sad
:|	Not amused
:||	Angry
:))	Very happy
:((	Very sad
:-D	Laughing
:-O	Surprise
:'-)	Crying
(:)	Bald
8–)	Wears glasses
=:)	Has a mohican/punk
;-)	Wink

These can be used to let the recipient know that the message is meant to be satirical or that you are upset, etc. These emoticons have become an established part of the E-mail community, and as you can see from some of the other icons shown, people have created many of them more for fun than for expressing emotion. Although it is quite acceptable to use these emoticons, there is another school of thought that believes these are unnecessary as letter writing has existed for centuries without the need for these symbols. Certainly, with some thought and consideration to the text of your message, it is possible to convey the meaning without resorting to these symbols – but this does remove some of the immediacy of E-mail.

These are the main guidelines for writing E-mails, but there are also some that cover how to deal with sending and receiving messages. These include dealing promptly with any messages received by E-mail, as many people choose to communicate by E-mail to ensure that you receive the message quickly – and therefore expect a prompt reply.

Two other guidelines, which appear to contradict each other, are that you should not forward private messages to other people and that you should not send anything via E-mail that you feel is too personal to be seen in public. These are really common sense, as you should always remember that E-mail is written in an open standard that can be read by any computer, and anything on the Internet is in the public domain. If you do want to send personal or sensitive information over the Internet, it is possible to buy encryption software which will make it more difficult (but not impossible) for unauthorised people to read you messages. However, if you do receive private or personal information from someone, you should respect that person's privacy. Great care should be taken when forwarding any message, as the style of the message tends to depend on the relationship between the sender and the recipient. If this message is forwarded to another individual, the style may not be appropriate for communication between the original sender and the new recipient – possibly giving rise to misunderstanding.

3 The World Wide Web

Introduction

The World Wide Web (WWW, Web, or W3) is the part of the Internet that has really caught the public's imagination. To many, the Web *is* the Internet, with the other services and protocols available serving only peripheral functions. It has been the main driving force behind the conversion of the Internet from a communication medium for technophiles and computer specialists to the global information provider for everyone that it has quickly become. The Web has provided an intuitive and graphical façade to the complex computer networking that makes Internet communication possible. This has changed the Internet from a user-unfriendly, text-based computer system that required the user to know the necessary commands to perform any action, into a system that is accessible to all and guides the user through processes using text, graphics, and sound.

This façade, or user interface, is ideal for allowing a user to browse through information and to follow a series of links to find the specific details they seek. The Web's user interface works so well that it has been adopted by Microsoft, the world's largest software company, as the interface for accessing core information within their computer operating systems. A user can find files and documents on their own PC or access helpful information about the software (using the 'help files') through a user interface modelled on that used to browse the Web. Another example of how the Web's influence has spread further than the Internet community is the explosive growth of corporate Intranets, which use web technology and techniques to disseminate information within organisations. The use of Intranets, and in particular the NHSNet, are covered in detail in later chapters.

The Web is one of the newest services on the Internet, but since its inception at CERN in 1989 it has become a hotbed of innovation, with new features and content appearing daily. It has developed from a method of disseminating and linking textual information into an important means of providing and receiving goods and services.

The protocol used by the Web is called HTTP, which stands for hypertext transfer protocol. The keyword is 'hypertext' as it describes a method of relating documents by inserting links to the relevant page from within the text of the document. The documents themselves are written in a computer scripting language called HTML (hypertext markup language), which enables the author to embed the links into the document.

How the Web works

The appeal of the Web over other Internet protocols is largely due to this ability to hide the complex communications behind the user-friendly interface. However, an understanding of how the Web works can help your use of the Web and help you to discern why things may be going wrong.

The Web uses the client/server method of information storage. This is a popular model for computer systems, with many networks built on this principle. This system differentiates between two types of computers – the client and the server. The server is the computer that stores the information and allows client computers to look at the information stored upon it. This means that the server has to be designed to allow a number of clients to access it simultaneously. In practice, this means that a server normally has a large amount of storage space on its hard disk, and a large amount of memory to allow fast access to the data stored on these hard disks. In Web terms, the server is the computer that holds the web pages, the client is the computer using the browser software. Each server can host a number of web sites, or a large site can be spread over a number of servers. In general terms, large organisations will have their own web server, and smaller organisations will rent space on a third-party's server as it is a major undertaking to maintain a server that is constantly connected to the Internet.

The client software used to access the web sites on the servers is called a browser, as it allows you to browse through the content of a server. The browser software is essentially very simple, as the web server undertakes the majority of the work. The primary task of the browser is to display the information sent from the web server, and it should also help you to move between different sites.

When you point your browser at a web site, either via a hyperlink or by entering the uniform resource locator (URL) directly into the address line, your computer (the client) connects with the server that hosts the relevant web site. The server then sends the HTML page you have requested over this connection, with any related components such as images, sound files, etc. Your computer stores these files on your hard disk, and your browser software displays the result. The time taken to copy the web page (including all components) is dependent on a number of factors.

- If the server has a poor connection to the Internet, or not a large enough connection (i.e. does not have enough bandwidth) to cope with the demand for the pages stored upon it, then any connection will be slowed down by this bottleneck.

- The client's connection speed and computer's specification will also have a great impact upon the time taken to download the page. A dial-up account using an old PC will be much slower than a leased-line connection using a modern, high-performance computer.

- If there are a large number of clients requesting information from the server simultaneously, it must share its time and processing power between all these clients. This results in each client's request for a web page taking longer to process as the server has less time to devote to processing each individual client's request.

- The time of day when the connection is made can also have a drastic effect on the connection speed. This is especially noticeable around 11 a.m. in the UK, when Internet users on the east coast of America start to come on line, with connection speeds degrading throughout the day as more of the US Internet user-base connects.

'Browser wars'

As detailed in Chapter 2, there are a large number of e-mail software packages, covering a wide spectrum of features and functionality. To access the World Wide Web you will probably use one of the two products that dominate the market – Microsoft Internet Explorer or Netscape Navigator. The battle for market dominance between these two packages and the companies behind them has been covered widely in the computer press and demonstrates the importance that Microsoft places on the Internet, and the Web in particular.

The browser market has tended to be dominated by one package for much of the Web's short history. This started in November 1993 when the first version of a package called NCSA Mosaic brought a graphical interface to web browsing, which had been a text-only affair until this time. However, a few of the original developers left to form their own software company, called Netscape, and produced their own browser called Navigator, which improved upon the standards set by Mosaic. As the market and the Web's user-base expanded, Netscape's Navigator took over as the dominant browser, helped by good marketing, including a free 90-day trial period and wide distribution via the Web. At this time the Internet went through its transformation from a network for computer technicians and academics into the global information resource. This is where Microsoft entered the browser market with their product, Internet Explorer. The marketing of Internet Explorer was extremely aggressive, with the product being distributed free of charge and supplied pre-installed on new PCs, where Microsoft enjoys a near monopoly with operating systems (i.e. the Microsoft Windows family of products) for new PCs. Microsoft's tactics brought it amazing growth, and also brought it to the attention of the US Department of Trade, who viewed this as anticompetitive behaviour. However, this has not stopped Microsoft making the Internet Explorer package an integral part of their operating systems from Windows 98 onwards. The result is that the ability to connect to, and use, the Internet has become a core feature of most PC operating systems, bringing the Internet within easy reach of the majority of computer users. Also, the integration of Internet tools has also occurred in other Microsoft products, including their popular range of application software including Word, PowerPoint, and Excel. This aggressive marketing and integration of Internet functionality demonstrates how the world's largest computer software company has identified the Internet, and especially the Web, as a key computer technology for the future.

It has also given rise to a new method of software distribution, by posting the latest version (or fixes for older versions) on their web site. A software company can achieve global distribution quickly and easily, with the majority of the distribution cost and time incurred by the users, therefore reducing the company's overheads. The new web-based distribution model has led to an immense increase in the amount of available 'shareware' (software that you can install and use for free, with a small fee paid to the author if you find it useful).

The basics

The software used to view documents on the Internet is called a 'browser' and this is a good description of how you view web-based documents, or 'pages'. When you call up a web page, you are seeing a document stored on a distant computer displayed in your browser's window. The page consists of blocks of text and links to images, sounds, small computer programs called 'applets', or other pages. Your browser will display the blocks of text and also follow the links to the images, sounds, or applets and display these on screen. If there is a link to another document, it will display this as underlined text in a contrasting colour to the rest of the text. The links to other documents are often referred to as 'hyperlinks'.

These hyperlinks are the foundation of the Web's ability to lead you to information, letting you follow a variety of paths to the same source document. This is also the reason why browsing the Web can be immensely rewarding, with information falling easily to hand, or immensely frustrating as you are led down blind alleys that take you away from the topic you seek.

Your browser can find the pages that are referred to by the hyperlinks as every page has a unique address.

Basic features of a web browser

The two major browsers (Microsoft Internet Explorer and Netscape Navigator) are very similar in function and features. The product life cycle for these packages is very short, with frequent updates becoming available via the Web. This means that any unique feature of one package quickly becomes standard in the rival. This frenetic pace of development has led to Netscape freely distributing the source code (the computer programming at the core of the software) for Navigator, to allow non-Netscape programmers to develop new features for the package. Therefore, the features detailed below are the principal and most frequently used facilities of these two browsers. When describing the features, the names used by Internet Explorer for each feature are used and the equivalent for Navigator are shown, where different. The features should also be present in any other browser package that you may use, although the names may differ.

Figures 3.1 and 3.2 are screenshots of Internet Explorer and

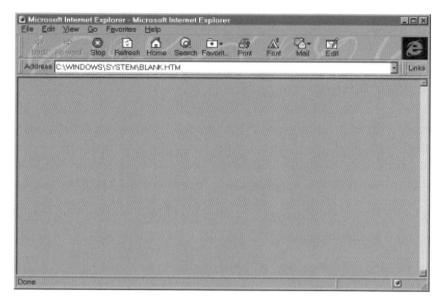

Figure 3.1 Screenshot of Microsoft Internet Explorer.

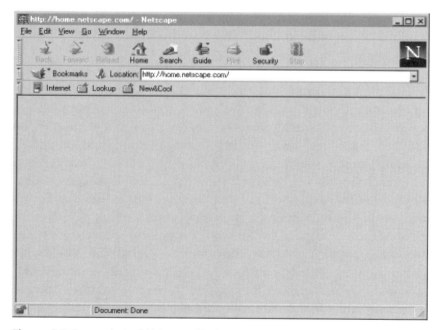

Figure 3.2 Screenshot of Netscape Navigator.

Netscape Navigator. As you can, see there is a large area where the web page is displayed, with a row of buttons and a space for an address (or URL) to be entered.

The main screen

A browser converts the HTML code of a web page into a readable format within the main screen. As the HTML code is an open standard, rather than the proprietary standards used by word processors, etc., a web page should be displayed in an identical manner by any browser. However, this is not always true, as the more recent or complex HTML codes have been interpreted in slightly different ways by Netscape and Microsoft. This has resulted in pages being displayed slightly differently by either browser package, with variances ranging from slight spacing differences to some components of web pages being ignored by one browser. Unfortunately, due to the continued development of new features and facilities, the differences between the packages appear to be on the increase. Some sites now require you to use either Netscape Navigator or Microsoft Explorer, but not the other, to view the pages correctly. A good web page designer will take into account the differences between the browsers and design their site to be displayed properly by both browsers.

The buttons

As with any modern Microsoft Windows–based software package, the most frequently used features can be accessed from buttons located on a toolbar. The principal buttons used by browsers are explained below.

The **Back** button is probably the most invaluable button on the browser's toolbar, as it will take you back to the previous page. As most web browsing involves following links to pages that may or may not lead to the information you are seeking, the ability to retrace your steps is a useful feature. It also ensures that you do not become stuck on a page that (through poor design) does not link to another page. The **Forward** button is the reverse of the Back button, allowing you to return to a page that you used the Back button to escape from.

The **Home** button allows you to return to your personal starting page, or 'home' page, from wherever you are on the web. Your home page is the initial page that is displayed when you start your browser, acting as your starting point for browsing the web. This means that if you become lost in the web, and too far down a series of hyperlinks to use the Back button, you can always return to your home page or starting point. A home page can also refer to the main menu or welcome screen of a web site. If you see a link to a home page within a web page, this will refer to the site's home page rather than your personal home page.

The home page can be set within the Options menu of your browser (from the View menu, select Options and the Navigation tab in Internet Explorer, and from the Options menu select General Preferences and Appearance in Navigator). When you install the browser software, your home page's default setting will be either Netscape's or Microsoft's web site. There has been growing competition between these companies and other Internet organisations to provide web users with their initial home page. These home pages or 'portals' are designed to provide the information and links most suited to your needs, while also generating advertising revenue for the organisation and links to pages the organisation wishes to promote.

The **Stop** and **Refresh** (or Reload) buttons are useful whenever there has been a problem in the transmission of the web page from the web server to your computer. The Stop button tells the remote computer to stop transmitting, allowing the web browser to concentrate on displaying the components of the page already retrieved. This can be useful when a web page contains a large graphic or any other large file, as the browser will not display the page fully until all the components of the page have been retrieved. By clicking on the Stop button, you can stop the download of the large image and then follow a link from any of those already displayed. Also, the browser will not allow you to exit the browser program while retrieving a web page, but by clicking on the Stop button the retrieval will be ended, allowing you to exit the package. The Refresh button will reload a page from the web server. This allows you to reload a web page which was not retrieved fully, either due to a problem in transmittal or when the retrieval has been stopped by the user. This can be especially useful at peak times, when pages can be partially retrieved or where there is a problem connecting to the web server referenced in the address (this normally appears as 'Connecting to *www.server.com* . . .' remaining in the status bar at the bottom of the screen for more than a few seconds).

The **Favourites** or **Bookmarks** button gives you access to your own personal collection of web addresses. One of the best ways to organise and store web addresses is by using this feature. Whenever you come across a site that you want to refer to in the future, you can add it to your list of favourites (or bookmarks). In Internet Explorer, you go to the Favourites menu and select Add to favourites. . . . In Navigator, you go to the Bookmark menu and select Add bookmark.

The **Print** button allows you to print the web page you are currently viewing. This is especially useful for forms or long documents that do not fit onto the screen. It is not uncommon to experience some problems printing web pages as they are designed for viewing on screen rather than printing to paper. Fortunately, both browsers have now been designed to cope with the common printing problems, giving users of version 4 onwards of either browser greater flexibility when printing.

The **Open** button appears only in Navigator, and can be used to enter the address or URL of the web page you want to visit. In Internet Explorer you can add this directly into the address line.

The address line

This is where the address or URL for the web page you wish to visit is shown. You can also enter an address into this space. From version 3 of both packages it is possible to omit the 'HTTP://' at the start of the address, as both packages will automatically assume that you wish to use the HTTP service to download the web page.

Additional features of browsers

The buttons on the browser toolbar provide access to the most frequently used features. However, there are other facilities built into Internet Explorer and Navigator that can enhance the use of the software.

Cookies

Web browsing normally involves viewing a web page located on a web server anonymously, with the server having no information regarding the person browsing the page. This makes it impossible for the web page to be tailored to the viewer, or for the web server to know how you arrived at its pages. This type of information could be very useful, and would allow a certain amount of two-way information exchange rather than the typical one-way communication from the server to the user. To facilitate this, your browser has a small text file called cookies.txt that a web server can access and add small lines of code to, called 'cookies'. These vary from storing an indication that you have visited the page previously, to a set of instructions that allow the web server to tailor the content of a web page to your interest areas. Probably the most popular use of cookies is to register visitors to a site, where the visitor must complete a registration form on their initial visit. The cookie is then created based on the registration details, and on subsequent visits the user is given direct access to the sites content. This allows the administrator of the site to gather useful demographic data about their site and also to monitor how frequently people return to their site. As the web server is accessing your computer and storing information upon it, there are security considerations. Because of this, most browsers will warn you that the web server wishes to give you a cookie, and will give you the option of stopping the passing of the cookie. In reality this option is due more to the perceived risk of cookies rather than any real risk of malicious information being stored upon your computer. The content of cookies is strictly controlled and defined and they can only be written in simple text due to the limitations of the cookie.txt file. Therefore you do not need to stop your browser from accepting cookies, but you may want to be informed whenever a web site tries to pass you a cookie. Both major browsers allow you to do this.

Frames

One of the most useful tools available to the web page designer is the ability to split the browser window into a number of separate screens or 'frames'. Each of these frames displays a different web page, and the option selected in one frame can influence the content displayed in another frame. When properly implemented this facility makes the navigation of a web site much easier and allows much greater flexibility in the display of information. Frames allow some parts of the screen to remain static while other parts of the screen are updated. A good example of this would be a contents page, where the contents page is displayed constantly while hyperlinks chosen from the contents frame change the web page displayed in the main frame. This makes it very easy to look quickly through all the pages referred to on the contents page without having constantly to reload the contents page.

Forms

Another feature that appears on some web pages are forms. These provide the visitor with the ability to add information into a web page, rather than just view the contents of the page. One of the most common applications of a form within a web page is a registration form, where the visitor enters personal information such as name and postal address. This allows the web site to gather information about visitors, giving the visitor an identity that is not normally provided by the relatively anonymous surfing of the Web. Other types of forms include visitor books or feedback forms, where visitors can provide useful information regarding their experiences of visiting a site, and simple multiple choice selection forms, where the visitor is offered a number of alternatives and can select the one that most suits their requirements. A very simple example of a form is that used to enter the criteria for a search engine, which consists of only one data entry box. Search engines are explained in Chapter 4.

Forms are becoming increasingly common as the commercial possibilities of the Web are realised, as there is an obvious need to know with whom you are dealing when providing a service via the Web. Another increasingly common application is for entering criteria for a search of a database of information, such as Medline. Applications like this allow the Web to become an excellent method of obtaining archive information.

Plug-ins

As the facilities of the Web have developed, the limitations of HTML are constantly being exceeded. This has resulted in the need for browser packages to understand types of computer files other than simple HTML documents. The simplest example of this is the need for the browser package to understand the different types of computer graphics file used on the Web, and also how to display these files. The browser has to contain converters or readers for these files so that it can understand what the file is and how to display it. However, the development pace of the Web is so fast with new types of multimedia files appearing on a regular basis, that it is impossible to build all of these converters into the software. Instead the browser packages use a modular approach, allowing you to add new converters or 'plug-ins' that can be used to read specific types of file. Some of the most common plug-ins are the Adobe Acrobat Reader, the Macromedia Shockwave player, and Progressive Network's RealAudio player. The Adobe Acrobat file format is used to distribute widely documents that can be read and viewed using the free Adobe Acrobat Reader, and is commonly used to distribute large text-based documents, such as reports and user manuals, via the Web. Macromedia Shockwave is a motion picture format, which can be played back using the free Shockwave viewer. A good example of a Shockwave 'movie' shows the life cycle of the AIDS virus and can be found at *http://www.roche-hiv.com/lifecycle/index.html*

RealAudio is a method of compressing or 'streaming' high-quality audio signals over the Web, and is the main method used to play music and provide speech via the Web to anyone with the RealAudio plug-in.

Java and JavaScript

Perhaps the most promising of the new developments in web technology is a computer programming language called Java, which has been developed by Sun Microsystems. Using this language, or the simpler scripting language called JavaScript, enables a web page to react to the user, rather than the static display associated with HTML. A web page designer can include 'applets' (small computer programs) within their web pages that perform certain tasks when triggered by an 'event' on the page. An event occurs when the user does something on screen, such as clicking on a button or moving the mouse pointer over a certain part of the page.

This has led to a wide variety of enhanced web sites, with Java or JavaScript being used for everything from buttons which change colour when pressed, to performing complex calculations based upon figures input by the user. Both Internet Explorer and Netscape Navigator have built-in support for Java from version 3 onwards.

Microsoft has developed a similar technology called ActiveX; it is not as widely used as Java/JavaScript but both browsers also contain support for its scripts.

The future of the Web

The Web has been the primary driving force behind the Internet's acceptance beyond the academic and technical communities, and this is almost certain to continue. Current developments in Internet technology are nearly all concerned with the Web and making the Web easier to use and easier to access. This means that the Web and the Internet will become synonymous and also much easier for the general public to use. The Web is the noisy upstart of Internet protocols, but it has established the Internet as an important communication medium for the twenty-first century.

Future technology advances that are discussed in more detail in Chapter 12 are likely to increase the availability of the Web and also to improve the content of web sites, bringing true multimedia experiences through high-quality video and sound. This means that the influence of the Web will expand further, making it an indispensable part of everyday life.

4 Searching the Web

Introduction

The anarchy of the Internet has allowed the wide proliferation of web sites catering for a wide variety of interest groups. However, this anarchy also makes it very difficult to find a specific web site, or the sites covering a particular interest. Without a method of categorising and ordering the vast number of available web sites, the task of finding the pages that interest you would be virtually impossible. Fortunately, this was realised very early on in the development of the Web and a number of indexes were created to organise the available web sites in a logical and structured format.

The initial indexes were little more than comprehensive lists of hyperlinks that were organised into a number of topics. The original index was the Virtual Library at CERN, which led to other enthusiasts setting up similar listings, including Yahoo, which was originally set up at Stanford University in the early days of the Web. The generic term for this type of index is 'directory listings'.

These original listings were maintained by enthusiasts who catalogued the sites that they visited. However, this would be an impractical approach for today's general interest indices, due to the vast number of new sites created daily that would need to be catalogued. Contemporary indices are maintained in a number of ways, such as users recommending the sites that should be added into a category or by using an automated scanning system that reads a web site and tries to categorise it based upon its content. The lists that are compiled using autonomous scanning agents, commonly referred to as 'robots' or 'spiders', maintain databases of the keywords found in scanned pages. These lists are called search engines, but this term is also often used to describe directory listings, as they perform the same function.

As the Web has developed, so the sophistication of search engines and directory listings has improved, making them an invaluable method of sifting through the vast amount of information available on the Web. This chapter covers the basic features of these search engines, and also shows you how to construct a simple search using a number of the available systems.

Paying for search engines

The original web site indexes were set up to help fellow users and were run either as hobbies or as research projects. As the Web has entered the mainstream, the search engines and directory listings have become full-time organisations, offering web searches as a commercial service. However, the cost of providing this service is not passed directly onto the user, as there is no charge for using the search facilities. These organisations generate their revenue through advertising and therefore whenever you use one of these services you will encounter 'banner' or 'click-through' advertisements. The advertisements appear on the top of the initial search criteria page, and subsequent search result pages, enticing you to click on the links to their web site. The web advertising industry is becoming more sophisticated and most search engines now tailor the advertisement you see to the keywords used in your search criteria.

Therefore, the use of search engines is free but you have to tolerate a relatively high level of advertising to benefit from the search services.

Directory listings versus search engines

As mentioned previously, there are two main type of index: the directory listing and the search engine. Both of these methods have their advantages and disadvantages but neither method is inherently superior. The best index for any given search will depend on the material for which you are searching.

The directory listing is reminiscent of a library catalogue, in which sites are grouped into categories and subcategories. This allows you to follow a defined path from a general heading through various subcategories before reaching the target area of interest. This is often referred to as top-down searching, as you start at the broadest scope of information before funnelling down into more specific areas. These directory listings are ideal when you are searching for sites that will fall into an easily discerned group, for example if you were looking for healthcare sites which specialised in cancer. Yahoo is probably the best-known directory listing and is one of the longest established and most comprehensive. Another leading directory listing is called Excite and it offers the same type of information as Yahoo, although it is not yet quite as comprehensive.

The alternative to the hierarchical structured organisation of the directory listing is the search engine, which relies on a database of sites referenced solely by their keywords. When using these engines, you insert the keywords, and the search engine returns all the pages that contain these words. This allows you to uncover useful sites that are either not registered in a directory listing or appear under a different, unrelated topic. These search engines rely on autonomous cataloguing programs that scan a web page and decipher the keywords and phrases from their content. These programs are often called 'spiders' or 'robots'. Search engines are better at finding a wide variety of sites compared to the directory listing. They can also be quicker if you know of a key phrase or word that you are searching for, as you do not need to navigate down through a list of directories and subdirectories. One of the leading search engines of this type is Alta Vista, which is run by Compaq, a leading computer system manufacturer. Another popular search engine is Infoseek.

Ranking

Search engines work by matching your key words or phrase against those found in the web pages contained within its database. At its simplest this would mean that any site that contained the keywords included in your criteria would be listed. However, if there are more than 100 sites that match your criteria, which is the norm for most searches, the sites which most closely match your criteria can become lost in the large number of sites that merely mention your keywords. To avoid this, the search engine will rank the matching sites, with the most relevant appearing at the top of the list.

The exact method of ranking for each search engine is slightly different, and is kept secret to prevent artificial boosting of rankings. However, there are a few basic principles which underpin the ranking systems of the main search engines. These are:

- the keyword is given higher priority if it appears in the title of the page
- the earlier in the text that the keyword appears, the higher the ranking
- the more often a keyword appears, the higher the ranking
- if the search criteria included a number of keywords, then the closer the proximity of these keywords, the higher the ranking

- if you have specified a number of keywords, the first specified word has precedence over the other words, the second keyword has precedence over the words after it, and so on; therefore pages that contain your first keyword have precedence over those pages that contain the last keyword.

The effect of these rules on your search criteria should be taken into account when deciding on your keywords. Based on these four ranking principles, it can be seen that if the keyword is in the title or is likely to be repeated, then these pages will appear earlier in the list of matching sites. Therefore, when constructing your search criteria you should aim to use words that are likely to appear at the beginning of the text and words with few synonyms. Also, you should consider how closely your keywords will appear in the text of the pages you are seeking, and try to use phrases or word combinations rather than a number of disparate keywords.

As the commercial aspects of the web have expanded, it has become increasingly important for companies to attempt to attain a higher ranking than their competitors. This has led to some web page designers using underhand methods to boost their ranking, such as using hidden text at the top of the page, which contains pertinent keywords repeated a number of times. To combat this, most search-engine providers monitor the cataloguing of pages and will exclude any that are blatantly abusing the ranking system.

By following these guidelines you should be able to improve the ranking of the sites you want to find, while reducing the number of irrelevant sites that appear high in the ranking. However, rogue sites, which appear to have no relevance to your search criteria, can still appear with a high ranking in the search results, either due to deliberate manipulation by the web page designer or through the keywords having an alternative meaning. Therefore, the ranking of sites should be taken as a guide rather than a definite statement on the relevance of a site. Also, it can be worth looking at sites that appear lower down the ranking.

Example searches

To demonstrate these four systems (Yahoo, Excite, Alta Vista, and Infoseek), the next section will show the results of two simple searches using all four indexes. The first search is to find pages that cover the medical condition keratoconus (a rare eye disorder) and the second will find organisations that are involved in the research or treatment of cancer. These two different searches have been chosen deliberately as the search engines should be better at finding sites dealing with a specific topic such as a medical condition, and by deliberately selecting an obscure condition the number of pages found should be relatively low. The search for cancer organisations should be better suited to the directory listings as they organise pages into categories and cancer is a broad and popular topic that should justify its own directory.

The two search criteria were selected before any searching was undertaken and therefore the results could not be predicted. The searches were conducted within approximately 1 hour on the same day in late 1998; however, such is the pace of change on the Internet, it is likely that the results would be different if the searches were undertaken even a few weeks later. These searches show that the results will vary between indexes, however, it should not be inferred that any particular system is better from these results as the two tests cover only a small subject area and were intended to show the difference between search engines and directory listings.

Search 1: keratoconus

As both the directory listings offer a search facility for their directories and this search was for a specific keyword, all four systems were searched using the keyword 'keratoconus'.

Alta Vista found 1864 web pages containing the keyword 'keratoconus', with the top five ranked pages being:

- Keratoconus and Cornea Transplants
  www.febo.com/eyes/
- Laser scan showing keratoconus
  www.plix.com/~users/dwollan/laser.htm
- Keratoconus Genetics Research Program
  www.laser-prk.com/keratoco.htm
- What is Keratoconus
  www.washingtoneye.com/keratoconus.html
- Keratoconus
  www.eugeneeyecare.com/of00018.htm

The other search engine, Infoseek, was next, with 543 results on the search for 'keratoconus', with the top five sites being:

- Genetic and Molecular Research in Eye Disease
  www.eyebirth-defects.com/surgical.htm
- PAR Vision Keratoconus Analysis
  www.cquest.com/russo/keratana.html
- KERATOCONUS & RESEARCH
  www.csmc.edu/nkcf/research.html
- Journal of Refractive Surgery
  www.slackinc.com/eye/jrs/vol115/9ra.htm
- Keratoconus Genetics Research Program
  www.keratoconus.com/

The Excite directory listing performed better than expected, finding 449 matches to 'keratoconus'. The top five were as follows:

- Tecor/Health & Fitness/Conditions & Diseases/Keratoconus – an Excite directory of sites dealing with keratoconus
- Keratoconus
  www.lowvision.org/keratoconus.htm
- National Keratoconus Foundation (NKCF)
  www.csmc.edu/nkcf/
- National Keratoconus Foundation (NKCF)
  www.csmc.edu/nkcf/default.html
- CIBA VISION – Keratoconus
  www.cvo-us.com/k.html

The Yahoo search on 'keratoconus' was the least successful, with a specific Yahoo 'category' (i.e. directory) called Health: Diseases & Conditions: Keratoconus devoted to the subject and containing three pages, plus another three pages in other categories that also mentioned keratoconus. Yahoo does not show the URLs of the sites, presumably as an attempt to use more user-friendly, plain English rather than the sometimes obscure codes used in URLs. The six pages were:

- National Keratoconus Foundation in Health: Diseases & Conditions: Organizations category
- National Keratoconus Foundation in Health: Diseases & Conditions: Professional Organizations
- National Keratoconus Foundation in Health: Diseases & Conditions: Keratoconus

- Keratoconus Information in Health: Diseases & Conditions: Keratoconus
- Keratoconus – holographic surface maps in Health: Diseases & Conditions: Keratoconus
- Dwyer, Dave and Joan in Society and Culture: People: Personal Home Pages.

The results show that the search engines, and in particular Alta Vista, performed significantly better at finding sites than the directory listings. An explanation of the close results of Infoseek and Excite is that both try to perform the dual role of directory listing and search engine, giving extensive keyword search facilities while still maintaining directory listings to some extent. A couple of noticeable occurrences include the duplication of the National Keratoconus Foundation's entry in the Excite results, with the two URLs varying slightly and probably pointing at the same page. The NKCF entry is also duplicated in the Yahoo results as they have registered their site in a number of directories. The other noticeable occurrence is the lack of correlation between the top five results for the first three systems. Although the top five results is a very small sample, it is surprising that one web page did not appear in the list of at least two of the systems.

Search 2: cancer organisations

For this example, the keywords of 'cancer' and 'organisation' were used in the Alta Vista and Infoseek search engines, while the following of links was used to find the correct directory with the Excite and Yahoo systems.

Yahoo was arguably the best for this search, with a relatively simple path through the topics of Health: Diseases and Conditions: Cancer leading to 68 web sites arranged in alphabetical order. These included:

- American Institute for Cancer Research
- The Anti-Cancer Foundation
- Asociacion Nacional Contra el Cancer – Panama
- Cancer Relief Macmillan Fund
- Imperial Cancer Research Fund.

The Excite directory listing also offered a relatively simple directory path of 'Health: Diseases & Conditions: Cancer & Hematology' (*sic*).

This led to a mixed screen offering further subdirectories covering specific types of cancer, e.g. breast cancer, leukaemia, and skin cancer, plus a few recommended web sites (including OncoLink) and a list of 41 'more sites' that covered a wide spectrum of cancer-related topics arranged in alphabetical order, with the titles of the organisations used rather than the URLs. These sites included:

- Association of Cancer Online Resources
- International Union Against Cancer
- National Cancer Institute
- University of London Institute of Cancer Research
- The Washington State Cancer Pain Initiative.

Infoseek also offered a mix of options when the search criteria '+cancer +organisations' was used. It found 700 matches to the criteria and also recommended a couple of directories, including Diseases & ailments: Cancer. This directory included 65 sites and the top five ranked sites were:

- CancerGuide Table of Contents
  www.cancerguide.org/mainmenu.html
- Children's Cancer Web
  www.ncl.ac.uk/nchwww/guides/guide2.htm
- InterNet Resources for Cancer
  www.ncl.ac.uk/#nchwww/guides/clinks1.htm
- National Cancer Institute (NCI)
  www.nci.nih.gov/
- National Cancer Institute: CancerNet Cancer Information
  www.cancernet.nci.nih.gov/

The top ranked sites from the keyword search were:

- National Alliance of Breast Cancer Organizations
  www.nabco.org/
- Y-ME National Breast Cancer Organization
  www.y-me.org/
- National Breast Cancer Coalition
  www.natlbcc.org/
- Avon's BCAC – Breast Cancer Support Groups
  www.pmedia.com/Avon/support.html

- EORTC Web Site
  www.eortc.be/

Finally, Alta Vista found 22 648 web pages that meet the criteria of '+cancer +organisations'. The top five ranking sites were:

- CancerWEB: Organisations: Gastrointestinal Cancer
  www.graylab.ac.uk/cancerweb/orgs/gastro.html
- CancerWEB: Organisations: Breast Cancer
  www.graylab.ac.uk/cancerweb/orgs/breast.html
- UK based Cancer Research Organisations
  christie.man.ac.uk/library/ukres.htm
- CancerHelp UK: Cancer Organisations
  medweb.bham.ac.uk/cancerhelp/public/orgs/typesof.html
- CancerWEB: Organisations: Lung Cancer
  www.graylab.ac.uk/cancerweb/orgs/lung.html

The directory listings provided the best results from this search by providing an easy to find list of relevant organisations. Although Alta Vista found the most pages, it can be seen that three of the top five pages related to specific pages within the same CancerWEB site. The other problem with the search engine results is that they do not differentiate between the organisations dealing with cancer and an organisation's page that deals with cancer. The Infoseek result demonstrate this, as the keyword results are dominated by breast cancer issues rather than the organisations involved in cancer treatment and research, such as the National Cancer Institute mentioned in Infoseek's own recommended site listing. The difference between the results found by Yahoo and Excite is relatively small, with Yahoo having slightly more sites registered. The facility to look into a particular type of cancer offered by the Excite results is available with Yahoo, but at a higher level.

These two searches have displayed the different strengths and weaknesses of search engines and directory listings. It can be seen that search engines provide noticeably better results when looking for specific words or phrases, whereas directory listings are better at finding sites covering a particular subject area or topic.

Boolean logic

When constructing a search, you need to use Boolean connectors to show the relationship between keywords. The three main terms are:

- AND – used to show that both words are required, e.g. public AND health would find pages that contained both these words and would ignore those that contained only public or only health
- NOT – used to show words that should be excluded, so *x* NOT *y* would find pages that contain *x* but do not contain *y*; for example, 'paddington NOT bear' would produce details of pages that referred to Paddington Station but not pages that referred to Paddington Bear
- OR – used when two keywords can substitute for each other, e.g. child OR paediatric would retrieve pages that contained either or both of these keywords.

Using a combination of these Boolean connectors within your keyword search can allow you to build complex search criteria.

The exact implementation of Boolean logic varies between search engines; for example, Alta Vista requires you to use AND NOT rather than NOT to identify keywords you wish to exclude. In general, when you add more than one keyword into the search box of a search engine it will assume that you want both words to be used, i.e. that the AND operator is being used.

Problems with search engines

Search engines and directory listings appear to provide the solution to the problem of locating information on the Web. They do make it possible and relatively easy to find information on the Web but they also suffer from a number of problems. These problems do not outweigh the advantages offered by a good index, but by understanding why things go wrong with search results it is possible to lessen the effect of these shortcomings and make more effective use of the available indexes. The following section explains the most common problems that affect all indexes to a greater or lesser extent.

Out-of-date links

One of the most frustrating problems when using search engines and directory listings is following a link and finding that the page no longer exists. This is a common problem due to the fast-changing environment of the Web. The search engines do check and remove redundant links; however, there can be a considerable time lag between the page disappearing and the link being removed.

Unfortunately, there is not an easy solution for this problem, although some web page designers do leave a link from the redundant page to the new location, which can be helpful in some instances. The only real solution is the Back button on the browser's toolbar.

Incomprehensible sites in the result ranking

In the early days of the Web, web pages were simple text-based documents. As the Web has developed, the structure of web pages has become more complex, with pages now containing the front-end of databases, or using small programs such as Java applets, etc. When you view these complex pages they appear in a comprehensible format; however, the underlying code consists of programming commands and syntax interspersed with text. The search engine 'spider' looks at the underlying code of a page rather than the content that appears in the browser window. Therefore, it reads and catalogues the computer programming. The result of this is that where the search engine displays the title and first few lines of the web page, more complex pages will appear to the user as an indecipherable jumble of computer programming codes.

Conclusion

Search engines make the navigation of the Web much easier and allow you quickly to narrow down your search for relevant material. The two main methods of categorising sites, directory listings and search engine robots, both have their advantages and disadvantages. The search engine excels at finding sites that contain keywords, whereas the directory listings are much better at collating sites concerning interest areas. Due to this, the majority of competing search services now offer a combination of the two approaches, allowing you to search the contents of the directory listings for keywords.

To make the most of keyword searching, you need to take your choice of keyword and the syntax used to a more advanced level. Another good method of making the best use of search results is to bookmark the most useful sites. The next chapter covers these features and more, allowing you to get the most of both search engines and directory listings.

5 Surfing and sifting

Introduction

The World Wide Web provides access to a mass of information covering a diverse range of subjects, both mainstream and alternative. It can be a goldmine of information, allowing you to track down an obscure fact or detail in minutes that would normally take weeks through more conventional sources. However, this great strength of the Web is also a weakness, as it is quite possible to overlook a valuable source of information due to the sheer quantity of options that are presented.

Most people's first impression of the Web is one of awe mixed with excitement at the possibilities presented, but for most users this is superseded quickly by questions on how to find the information that is relevant or of interest to them. This chapter aims to show some of the methods that can be used to filter the information that bombards the user and how to separate the wheat from the chaff.

Advanced search techniques

The previous chapter dealt with simple searches using search engines and directory listings. As this showed, it is quite easy to carry out a search that produces more pages than you can realistically examine. To reduce the number of hits produced to a reasonable level, it is possible to take the construction of your search criteria to a more advanced level. Refining your search by including and excluding other keywords can do this, or it can involve limiting the search to specific criteria other than keywords.

Wildcards

One of the easiest ways of improving a search is to use wildcards to ensure that the variety of spelling options and tenses are included in your search. The normal wildcard character is an asterisk (★) and this is used to denote that any character or number of characters is acceptable in this position. For example, paediat★ would include paediatric, paediatrics, paediatrician, etc.; whereas if paediatric is specified, all references to paediatrics and paediatrician, etc., would be ignored. This has obvious benefits in ensuring that all connotations of a word are included in the search and that all occurrences in a page are counted and contribute to the page's ranking.

Capitalisation

As mentioned previously, if a word is capitalised a search engine will ignore all instances of a word where it is written in lower case. If, however, the word in the search criteria is written in lower case, all occurrences of the word will be included in the search results regardless of whether the word appears capitalised or not. Therefore capitalising a word in the search criteria can restrict the search to only capitalised versions of the word. This can be a good way of refining a search or it can exclude valid pages unnecessarily, depending on the circumstances. For example, a search for 'Bob AND Hope' would produce a very different result to a search for 'bob AND hope'.

Phrases

By using keywords in a search the search engine will count every occurrence of each individual keyword. However, it is sometimes the case that the best keyword for a search is not a single word but a phrase. For example, if you wanted to find information about artificial limbs the simple search would count 'we went out on a limb and used artificial flowers' as a good match against the criteria. Therefore it can be quite useful to indicate that words should appear adjacent to one another. This is done by encapsulating the phrase in inverted commas, i.e. "artificial limb".

Domain restrictions

Another refinement that is suited to some situations is to restrict the domains to be included in a search. As most (but not all) British organisations are registered under the UK domain it is possible to restrict a search to only UK registered sites, or to any other country-based domain, such as France or Australia, etc. The method of implementing this varies between search engines, with the easiest probably being Yahoo where you can restrict the search to sites within their UK & Ireland directory lists. In Alta Vista it can be added to the search criteria by adding the domain: prefix, e.g. 'clinic★ AND audit AND domain:uk' would restrict a search to UK sites. Another useful feature within the Alta Vista search engine is to restrict the language to English, therefore eliminating sites written in French, German, etc.

Refining searches

Most search engines allow you to refine an existing search to remove the less relevant sites from the search results. Again the implementation of this will vary between the search engines, with the quality of support also varying.

In Alta Vista it is possible to refine a search using options provided by the search engine. By selecting the refine option it will take you into a screen that groups other commonly found keywords that have appeared in the pages from your search criteria. These groups can then be included (equivalent of entering AND in the search criteria) or excluded (equivalent of NOT) in your search criteria. This allows you to refine your search, however the selection of other possible keywords can often lack 'intelligence' in that they have little or no relevance to the context of your search.

Organising bookmarks

As mentioned in Chapter 3, the bookmark facility is one of the most useful features included with your web browser. This works as a web page address book, allowing you to record the address of pages that you visit frequently and to access the page straight from the relevant entry in your address book. In Netscape Navigator these are called bookmarks, whereas Internet Explorer refers to them as favourites.

In both packages you can access any address contained with your bookmarks quickly by clicking on them from the drop-down menu provided. However, if you use the Web frequently you will soon build up a long list of bookmarks that will become difficult to manage. Therefore it is important to organise your bookmarks into categories and to store them in subdirectories rather than as one long list.

Another important part of organising your bookmarks is to ensure that the entry in your bookmark file is given a memorable name. Problems can occur with the naming of your bookmarks, as your browser will automatically use the title of the web page as the bookmark's title. Normally this gives a good description of the page; however, some sites have badly titled pages, giving rise to obscurely named references in your bookmark file. Therefore it is always worth checking the title given to the entry when it is added to your bookmark list to ensure that it is memorable and descriptive.

'Related sites' host sites

The early search engines did not use robots to categorise sites but relied on enthusiastic web users producing pages listing the sites they had visited and sharing this list with other web users. With the massive growth that the Web has experienced, it would be virtually impossible for an individual or small group of enthusiasts to produce a list of sites covering the wide spectrum of topics included in the original search engines. However, a number have produced listings covering their particular area of interest, either with altruistic motives or as an attempt to generate return visits to their own sites.

These normally take the form of a relatively small list of closely related sites, with up to about 50 links to other sites listed on one page on the web site. This type of page is normally labelled as a 'useful links' or 'other sites' page and can also occasionally give a brief summary of the linked site or just the full name of the site.

Other sites take a more professional approach offering either a more complete list of sites organised into subsections, such as *http://drdesk.sghms.ac.uk/* which 'seeks to be the ultimate home page for general practice'. Other sites offer more dynamic lists, aiming to provide visitors with details of the latest sites or pages containing information regarding their specialist area, such as the Dr Harry column on the NHSNet. Some other examples of these sites include:

- *http://www.shef.ac.uk/uni/academic/R-Z/scharr/netting.htm* — the 'Netting the Evidence' page provided by the Sheffield Centre for Health and Related Research that covers medical-research-related sites.

- *http://www.gwent.nhs.gov.uk/trip/* — this is the Turning Research Into Practice (TRIP) site, which centres on evidence-based medicine but also gives a guide to other medical sites.

- *http://www.pslgroup.com/drsguide.htm* — this is a commercially run site that provides news and alerts about a number of medical conditions and also provides a list of related sites for each condition.

These sites can offer useful links to sites that may be of interest, allowing you to benefit from the time spent by other healthcare professionals searching the Web for information. By using these types of sites and bookmarking them for future reference, you can gain a useful shortcut to information.

Other useful sources of web page addresses are the more traditional media of magazines and journals. Many journals now contain a column that covers web sites related to their content, giving a brief summary of the site and also the URL. These are very useful when trying to find sites about a specific subject, as the journal for that topic will concentrate on web sites related to the subject area, with less attention paid to the sites covering peripheral subjects.

Understanding web page URLs

As explained in Chapter 1, every web page has its own unique URL, which is based on the page owner's domain name. However, it is a frequent occurrence on the Web, especially when using search engines, for a web page URL to not be found. There are a number of reasons for this, including mistyped URLs and pages no longer existing. However, it is possible to find pages that at first appear to no longer exist. To do this you need to understand how URLs for an individual page are constructed, and how they are stored on the web server.

Using the 'Netting the Evidence' page listed above (*http://www.shef.ac.uk/uni/academic/R-Z/scharr/netting.htm*) as an example, you can see that the page is contained within the shef.ac.uk domain (this is Sheffield University's registered domain). The construction of domain codes was dealt with in Chapter 1, but for this section the rest of the URL is of more interest.

Just as computer files on your computer are stored in directories and subdirectories, the files on a web server are stored in a similar manner. One difference to note is that on a PC computer the character used to denote a directory name is '\' whereas web servers use the '/' symbol. In this example you can see that the address contains four directories (*uni*, *academic*, *R-Z*, and *scharr*). This leaves the final part of the URL – *netting.htm* – that refers to the actual web page. Nearly all web pages will have the suffix of *.htm* or *.html* as this denotes a file saved in HTML format. Some page URLs do not show an html file, such as the TRIP site's *http://www.gwent.nhs.gov.uk/trip/* – this is due to every web server having a specified filename that will load auto-matically if someone accesses a directory upon it, commonly referred to as the default page. The two most common filenames are default or index with the htm or html suffix (e.g. *index.html*). Thus if you access the TRIP web site using the above URL, the default page will be loaded.

Therefore, if you try to access a web page with a URL ending in *.htm* or *.html* and the page is not found, it is often worth trying the address without the filename on the end. This should load the default page if the directory still exists. If a file does not load automatically but a list of filenames does appear, you should look for a file called index or default and follow the link to it. If a file is still not found, the next step is to try one directory higher in the address, and continuing until you are left with just the domain name. Using the Sheffield address, this would mean that, if the address, *http://www.shef.ac.uk/uni/academic/R-Z/scharr/netting.htm*, was unsuccessful, you could remove the *netting.htm* from the end to see whether a page appeared. If not, the next step would be to try *http://www.shef.ac.uk/uni/academic/R-Z/* – to see whether this produced a result. This could be followed by *http://www.shef.ac.uk/uni/academic/* and then *http://www.shef.ac.uk/uni/* and finally *http://www.shef.ac.uk/* to see if a page appeared.

Another consideration is the use of capitalisation, as most web servers treat a capital 'R' as a separate letter from 'r'. Using the Sheffield URL again, if the address was entered as *http://www.shef.ac.uk/uni/academic/r-z/scharr/netting.htm* instead of *http://www.shef.ac.uk/uni/academic/R-Z/scharr/netting.htm* it is likely that the page would not be found.

Cache

When you follow a link from a web page, the next time you return to the original page the hyperlink is shown in a different colour, to denote that you have followed this link. The browser software can identify the pages that you have visited previously, as it stores these pages in its cache. When you are using the Web and go to a new page your web browser checks to see if the relevant page is stored in its cache and loads it from here if it is available. Only if the page is not cached does your browser connect to the relevant web site and download the page. This happens transparently for the user, with the only noticeable difference being the speed that cached pages are loaded in comparison to those retrieved across the Web.

The cache stores a copy of these pages and the associated graphics, etc. that were linked to the page on your computer's hard disk. The browser can also ensure that the cached copies of pages are kept up to date by checking whether the cached pages are still the most recent versions. The aim of the cache is to reduce the amount of time spent downloading frequently visited pages, as the page is stored locally, only communicating with the remote computer to check whether the page has been updated. Therefore, it is worthwhile maintaining as large a cache as possible without degrading the performance of your own computer. A cache that is too large will become obvious when you exit your browser, as this is when the maintenance of the cached files is undertaken. A large cache takes much longer to clear, and therefore there will be a noticeable delay between the request to close the browser and the browser completely exiting.

In Internet Explorer, the cache is called the 'history' and can be modified to store the history of pages browsed over a set period of days. To adjust the number of days that are stored in the history, you can go to the View menu and choose Options. At the bottom of the navigation screen you can then modify the number of days stored in the history file and also view the files stored there or delete all records from the history file.

In Navigator, the cache stores all pages until a set amount of the computer's hard disk is filled. To edit these settings you can go to the Options menu and select Network Preferences. On the cache screen you can set the maximum size of the memory cache and disk cache. The memory cache gives even quicker access to pages browsed in the current session and is cleared automatically whenever you exit Navigator. Increasing the size of the memory cache will have a more drastic and noticeable effect on your computer system's performance. Netscape also allows you to choose when the package checks for a more current version of the cached page on the Internet. You can choose to check once per session, which means that it will check the first time you load the page during a browsing session, or you can select every time, which means it will check every time you load the page. And finally, you can select never, where it does not check for a more recent version of the page (this option is not recommended).

You can speed up your average web browsing session significantly by increasing the size of your cache, as many of your favourite sites will be accessed quickly from the cache. However, the size of the cache is limited by the size of your hard disk and it is quite easy to fill the cache with a few days worth of pages. To overcome this shortcoming there are a number of extensions to cache available.

Proxy servers

If your Internet connection is shared with colleagues within your organisation it is fairly likely that your caches will contain a number of duplicate web pages as your interests will be similar and will lead you to similar sites. Therefore, it would reduce the time spent searching the Web and reduce the traffic onto the Internet if your organisation had a shared cache. This would mean that the first user to visit the site would load the web page from the Internet, whereas subsequent colleagues would only need to retrieve it from the local cache. The software to enable this is widely available and is usually called 'proxy server' software, because it serves as an intermediary between your browser and the Internet as all requests for pages are routed through the proxy server. Both Microsoft and Netscape offer a proxy server as an add-on for their popular web-server software.

The advantages of providing a shared cache to a group of users is not limited to within an organisation as the same rules can be applied to the Internet community as a whole. As the web sites on the Internet vary widely in their popularity, it makes sense for an ISP to provide a cache of the more popular sites for its subscribers. Therefore most ISPs provide a proxy server for their subscribers to access and it is an important consideration to make when selecting your ISP.

To utilise a proxy server, you need to point your browser to look up web pages on it before retrieving the page from the Internet. To do this you need to know the URL or IP address of the proxy server (this should be supplied by the administrator of the cache – either your ISP or IT department. In Internet Explorer, you need to select the Internet Options from the View menu. On the connections page you will find a proxy server section that allows you to specify the location of the proxy server. In Navigator, you need to go to the advanced section of the Preferences menu and select the Proxy option. The details of your proxy server can be entered under the 'Manual Proxy Configuration' option.

If your organisation or ISP does not support a cache, it is still possible to gain access to one as various web sites offer a cacheing system for its visitors. To obtain a list of these web sites you can visit the *www.lightspeed.de/irc4all/eproxy.htm* web page for a detailed list. When selecting a site from this list it is advisable to select the site closest to you, as selecting a distant computer can degrade the performance of your web browser due to the distance each request to the cache must travel.

Although web cacheing provides better download speeds to the user, there are drawbacks to the system. These include the unnecessary duplication of web pages on all these proxy servers, which contradicts one of the great benefits of the Internet in that there is only one source of a web page, thus ensuring accuracy and timeliness. Another potential problem is that once a page is held in cache it is possible for it to be changed without the knowledge of the original author, which raises concerns over the accuracy and authenticity of the information. Therefore it can sometimes be useful to ensure that the page you access is the one located at the URL specified rather than a cached copy of the page. To force your browser to retrieve the original document you can press the Shift key and click on Refresh while viewing the relevant page.

Mirror sites

Another method of increasing access speeds to popular sites is to mirror the site at another location. This involves maintaining two or more identical web sites throughout the world, with web browsers pointed towards the site nearest to them. This not only speeds up access, as the data exchanged between the site and the user has to travel a shorter physical distance, it also shares the load between a number of sites, thereby easing the load on each individual server. Probably the most popular pattern of locations for mirror sites is one in the US and one in Europe (reflecting the high usage in both these areas), and perhaps a third site in the Far East/Pacific Rim.

Non-medical sites

Although the emphasis of this chapter, and the book, is the medical information available upon the Internet, there is also a wide range of useful information services available that are not related to medicine or health.

There is a wide variety of information available, and as more companies realise the benefits of using the Web to provide services, rather than as a place to display promotional material, the number of useful sites will increase. Listed below are two British sites that provide invaluable advice to the traveller, and exemplify how the Web can be used to give access to information in ways that would be impossible through traditional media.

- *www.railtrack.co.uk* is run by Railtrack, the company responsible for maintaining the railway network in the UK. This site offers a really useful timetable database, which allows you to discover quickly the times, and the changes required, of the trains between your starting location and your destination. For example, if you wanted to travel between Bradford and Bournemouth you could find out the time of the first train after your chosen departure time (e.g. next train after 2 p.m.). It can also tell you what time you would need to leave Bradford if you wanted to arrive in Bourne-mouth at a certain time. What makes this system stand out is that the timetable covers all train operators and therefore all trains.
- *www.rac.co.uk* is the Royal Automobile Club's web site and offers live traffic information. This gives you the latest information about any accidents or roadworks that could affect you in the selected area of the country. This information is constantly updated so you can be certain that it is the latest news regarding traffic problems.

Two of the most quoted examples of good commercial sites that show how a well-designed web site can provide tailored services to the customer are those run by Dell computers (*www.dell.com*) and the Amazon bookstore (*www.amazon.com*). The Dell site allows the visitor to buy a new PC built to his or her own specification, and also allows you see the latest price. This is particularly important for computers, where prices are constantly updated, changing at least every month. The Amazon site takes this even further, as the regular visitor is provided with their own custom web page showing the latest offerings in their areas of interest. Amazon will also E-mail you with details of newly arrived books in your chosen subject area. For the less-frequent visitor, the Amazon site still allows you to find all the books about any subject area very quickly and quite intuitively, giving you a list of available books that surpasses the offerings of even the largest conventional bookshop.

Conclusion

Using advanced search techniques and favourites to find the pages that cover your particular interest area, and by optimising the set-up of your browser and Internet connection, it is possible to make efficient use of the services available on the Web. However, part of the appeal of the Web is the numerous other information sources and services which are initially interesting and quickly become essential tools for gaining information. The Web offers information in new and innovative ways, and allows you to search globally rather than in the narrow range offered by traditional media. What makes this information source even more exciting is that it is still in its infancy, and new developments promise to make higher-quality information available while requiring less effort to retrieve. At present it is possible to become overloaded by the information possibilities of the Web and care needs to be taken when evaluating the quality of information presented. The methods available to evaluate web pages are dealt with in the next chapter.

6 Validity and security

Introduction

The Internet is a good source of information regarding a wide range of medical subjects. However, people lacking medical expertise, such as patients or their relatives, very often create medical information sites and therefore the information found may be false or biased.[1] As anyone can create a web site on the Internet, and it is impossible to stop these people from posting inaccurate information regarding medicine or any other subject, it is important to filter the poorly informed sites from the valuable and accurate resources that are also available. This chapter looks at methods of filtering this information and how to evaluate the content of a web site. It will also look into the related subject of ensuring that good information is kept secure and how access to sensitive information can be restricted, as it is quite easy to corrupt accurate information if it is not properly secured.

Other media

The problem of inaccurate or misleading medical information is not a new problem and is it not limited to the Internet. Newspapers and TV are both possible sources of poor-quality information that can raise the public's concern about a number of subjects, and health-related stories are a popular topic due to their wide-ranging appeal. However, this does not mean that all information that appears via the mass media is inaccurate, and therefore each story must be evaluated separately.

Because these information sources are unreliable, it is impossible to trust or ignore totally the information that appears from them. If a story cannot be dismissed after an initial browse, it becomes important to find a corroborating source that consolidates the information provided. This corroborating source, or the initial story, must also provide some evidence to show that it is not based purely on the author's opinion.

Due to this need for corroboration and research to prove the value of the information, the scientific press undertakes this review of material before publication through a refereeing process. Therefore the reader of an article within the *BMJ* or *Lancet*, etc. can be confident that the information has some basis in scientifically undertaken research unless otherwise indicated.

Therefore, the initial evaluation of the accuracy of information is based upon the source, with greater importance given to the information coming from a source known to be reliable. The same situation relates to textbooks, including reference books, that can vary in the accuracy and comprehensiveness of contents, and therefore the reader must look for clues as to the likely reliability and objectivity, e.g. is it a reference book or a proponent of new ideas, in order to assess how to use the material. The author's identity and qualifications, publisher's reputation, independent foreword, and critical reviews in the press are also useful guides to the validity of information contained within a publication.

Web-site evaluation

These methods of evaluation can be applied successfully to most web sites, as the source of the information is normally apparent. Therefore it can normally be assumed that information appearing on the BMA's (British Medical Association's) site is more reliable than that appearing on an individual's home page. One of the quickest and easiest methods of evaluating a web site is to look at the URL of the site. This can show whether the page appears on a known and respected organisation's web site, an unknown organisation's site, or if it is a personal web site as provided free of charge by most ISPs.

However, this simple method of evaluation is not foolproof, as it is quite easy for an individual to register an impressive sounding URL and to design a site that appears to the visitor as an authoritative source of information. Also, most universities provide information resources that can be valuable to the researcher; however, these universities also tend to allow their students the opportunity to put information onto the Internet. Therefore it is quite possible for a university's site to contain both high-quality and poor-quality information, making it difficult for the visitor to know which is which.

Another problem is that due to the global nature of the Internet, it is as easy to access information on an Australian medical journal's web site as it is to access a British site. As it is impossible to know the review policies of all the journals available via the Web, it becomes difficult to evaluate the quality of the information displayed by international sources

However, by ignoring those sites that are provided by unknown sources you are limiting your options and negating many of the benefits the Web has to offer. It is also quite possible that an individual's site may contain valuable information and insights into the particular health issue that their site addresses.

Therefore, other techniques need to be used in conjunction with the evaluation of the web site's URL to determine the accuracy of the information displayed.

Other evaluation techniques

The other techniques used to evaluate web sites are also based on methods that are used to judge the content of other media. As most medical research is based upon work undertaken by others, there should be some indication of the work undertaken by these other bodies, in the form of references or hyperlinks to the relevant site. This applies to medical organisations' sites and those produced by patients or relatives, as it is important for both to show where they obtained their information. The Web was created with the idea of linking the various research projects undertaken at CERN, and a web page should make it easy for a visitor to jump to the referenced material via a hyperlink. By linking to the referenced information it also allows the visitor to see whether the original site has misrepresented the information, either deliberately or in error, thereby reinforcing or undermining the validity of the information stored on the original site.

One of the major benefits of the Web is that a site can be updated quickly to ensure that information displayed is always accurate and up-to-date. This has obvious benefits in the dissemination of medical information as the latest research can be distributed easily. However the Web also acts as a repository of archive information, allowing quick and easy access to large volumes of historical information. These two separate functions can cause problems when trying to find out information, as it can be difficult to ascertain whether the web page displays current or archive details. Therefore, web pages should be marked with the date that they were last updated, and this should give some indication of how current the information is. Unfortunately the majority of sites still omit this useful piece of information.

Alongside the last date of amendment, the page should show the author's name. This is another helpful indicator of the validity of the information. These points − explicit authorship and sponsorship, attribution of sources, and dating of material − were criteria that Silberg *et al.* proposed.[2] By using these criteria when constructing a web site, it is possible to demonstrate to the visitor the basis, timeliness, and ownership of the information contained within the site.

Another useful indicator about the information, which is alluded to by Silberg *et al.* is the purpose of the site and who has provided the financial backing or sponsorship of a site. Although much is made of how easy it is to publish on the Internet, there must still be a reason why that organisation or individual has made the effort to publish the material. The two main reasons are the altruistic motive, where there is a genuine desire to share this information to aid people in a similar situation, and a commercial motivation, where the information is published to promote the author or their organisation. Both motives can produce either good or bad sites, as the altruistic site can be a good source of well-researched information about a certain medical condition or it can be a misinformed and biased guide to a particular problem that concerns the author. Commercial sites can also suffer in the same way, as they may be thinly disguised promotional materials for the organisation's products or services. On the other hand, they can be well-researched and unbiased sites where the organisation seeks to associate itself with an authoritative source of information and so increase the perceived quality of its own products and services. Therefore when evaluating a site it is worth looking at whether the site falls into the altruistic or commercial category and the reason for publishing the material.

These criteria are also reflected in the principles for medical information web sites laid out by the Health on the Net (HON) organisation (*www.hon.ch*). This is a non-profit making organisation that was founded by an international initiative to promote the use of Internet technology within medicine and healthcare. The principles promoted by HON cover the criteria of explicit authorship, disclosure of sponsorship, etc., and also that any medical information is written by clinicians and is intended as support material to the doctor–patient relationship, rather than to replace this relationship.

There are also a number of other projects run by HON, such as a medical search engine (MedHunt) and a reference database of medical conference proceedings, etc., to promote responsible Internet usage.

Reference sites

As discussed in Chapter 5, it is possible to search for relevant sites in a number of ways, including the use of search engines and via 'related sites' pages on web sites. One of the easiest methods of reaching information that is known to be reliable is through the related sites page of a trustworthy organisation. By using this approach you can avoid the investigations needed to evaluate a web page, as the owner of the related site page has already undertaken this work.

The Organising Medical Networked Information (OMNI) Project is perhaps the best example of this, as all resources entered into OMNI are assessed for quality and regularly reviewed on the basis of detailed guidelines for selection and evaluation. The OMNI service is funded by the Joint Information Systems Committee of the Higher Education Funding Councils and is managed as part of the Electronic Libraries Programme (eLib), with the National Institute for Medical Research Library as the leading body. The URL is *www.omni.ac.uk* and there is also a mailbase mailing list available that E-mails details of the latest additions to you. The Cochrane Collaboration also has a web site for the dissemination of information regarding healthcare, and can be a valuable source of information for medical professionals and the public. This site has numerous mirrors across the globe, and the URL for the UK site is *www.update-software.com/ccweb/*.

Search engines are the easiest way to find a number of sites about a given topic; however, the mainstream search engines perform no verification of the sites registered with them and bear no responsibility for the information contained within them. This is quite obvious with Alta Vista and its ilk, due to their categorisation of sites by the words contained within them. However, the directory listings are the same, as there are no exclusion criteria to prevent any site from registering under the medical organisations directory. Therefore it is quite likely to find poor information sites registered under what appears to be an appropriate subdirectory. As mentioned in the previous section, The Health on the Net (HON) search engine, MedHunt, does validate sites, and the Medical World Search facility (*www.mwsearch.com*) also assesses sites before adding them to their database, ensuring that every site listed has been passed by their editorial board. These sites are categorised using the unified medical language system, which allows medical professionals (and other visitors) to search for sites based upon specific medical terms.

On-line databases and archives

Although the preceding part of this chapter has dealt with the validation of web-based content, it is important to remember that the Web is also a good source of archive information from other prevalidated sources.

Many respected medical journals and library sources maintain an archive of past information that can be accessed easily through their web site. A good example of this is the *BMJ*, who provide access to past issues and organise their archive under searchable headings. Therefore it is possible to go to the *BMJ* site and quickly obtain a list of articles that have dealt with a particular issue and view the content of these articles. Other available sources include reference libraries, such as Medline.

Notwithstanding concern over the quality of information presented on the Web, it is important to remember that it is also an invaluable tool for searching old information from more traditional media.

Security

When evaluating a web page, much of the emphasis is placed upon the reputation of the source, therefore you need to be certain that the source organisation or individual placed the information displayed there. Unfortunately it is possible for the contents of a web page to be altered or defaced without the author's knowledge. A notorious example of this was the altering of the Labour Party's web site, with Tony Blair's photograph replaced by a Spitting Images caricature. This was a very obvious example of an outside force altering a web page, but more subtle changes of the medical information contained within a 'respectable' site could have more far-reaching implications.

To alter the information within a web page, the hacker needs to gain access to the web server computer that stores the web page. To fully protect a web server from outside attack is difficult, due to the fundamental openness of the Internet standards. However, by reviewing the security policy regularly and monitoring the publicised flaws in the web-server's software, it is possible to maintain a high level of security. This is one of the primary reasons for arranging your web site through a commercial ISP, as they have the resources and technical staff to undertake this work.

Securing the Intranet

To secure an Intranet web server is an easier task, as the system is hidden from the Internet. If the Intranet offers access to the Internet, as the NHSWeb does, then this link to the Internet needs to be guarded. The most common protection is the use of a firewall, which sits between the Intranet and Internet and monitors the traffic passing through it. If any of this traffic contravenes the rules that govern the firewall, it will not be allowed to pass through.

The Intranet also offers greater physical security, as the location of all the computers that have access are known. This provides the opportunity to implement all the necessary security measures to provide a secure entry point onto the Intranet. This not only covers measures such as username and passwords but also non-computer-based steps, such as door locks and alarm systems.

These steps can be taken to secure access to the Intranet; however, it is impossible to ensure that all web site visitors meet the minimum requirement. Therefore other measures need to be taken to secure the information displayed upon the Internet that concentrate on the web site and the web server, as these are the only parts of the Internet that you control directly.

Secure sites

It is possible to make information available to selected people via the Internet or Intranet, but not to the general public. This allows the organisation to benefit from the universal access and ease of use of the Web for their sensitive information in addition to their public domain-information.

The most popular method of providing this security is to restrict access to authorised users via usernames and passwords. This is the normal method used to secure local area networks and can also be applied to a web site. The effect of this is to ensure that anyone who wishes to access the web site, or certain parts of the site, needs to log in using their username and password. This approach is not only used by sites containing sensitive information but is being used increasingly by commercial sites that offer value-added services to registered users who must pay a registration fee.

Some sites allow visitors to register their own usernames and passwords before accessing the site. This is not really a security measure as access is open to all, but does allow the web site administrator to gain information about the visitors to the site.

Encryption

Another major security concern is ensuring that information is not intercepted while being transmitted between secure sites. As it is relatively simple to capture Internet transmissions and to decipher the contents, there is an obvious need to encrypt the information exchanged between sites. This not only applies to sensitive or confidential medical information, but also to commercial data. One of the driving forces behind encryption is the need to provide a secure means of transmitting credit card details to enable the purchase of goods and services online, i.e. e-commerce.

Another method of securing web sites is the secure socket layer (SSL) that is supported by both of the leading web-browser packages. Both packages provide a visual clue to the user to indicate whether a site is secure, in the form of a key symbol. The key appears whole when accessing a secure web site, and broken when using an unsecured one. If SSL is implemented, the web server encrypts the web page and your browser decodes this on download. To the user this all happens transparently, but anyone trying to intercept the data for the web page will receive a garbled message.

Further developments that aim to provide web site visitors assurance that a site is secure and will preserve their privacy and personal details include the Platform for Privacy Preferences (P3P) Project run by the World Wide Web Consortium. This project is developing a specification that will enable web sites to express their privacy practices.[3] This will allow visitors to decide whether they trust the site enough to divulge their personal details. The software for this should soon be integrated into browser packages and web-server software, and will reassure users about their ability to share personal information with web sites

With E-mail, the process of encryption is much easier as the recipient is known, and there are several available means of securing E-mail transmissions. The main method of securing E-mail is to encrypt the messages and then provide the recipient with the code to remove the encryption. This is called 'public-key' encryption as the code unlocks the real message from the encrypted original. The major obstacle in the way of widespread use of encrypted E-mail is the US government, which has prohibited the export of advanced encryption algorithms in a bid to stop E-mail being used to spread illegal information that cannot be intercepted and read by their security services.

However, it is still possible to have secure E-mail over the Internet using the S/MIME standard that is being widely adopted by all the major E-mail software vendors. This is an extension to the MIME (multipurpose Internet mail extension) standard used with E-mail attachments.

References

1 Forsstrom J (1997) Why certification of medical software would be useful. *Int J Med Informatics* **47**:143–52.
2 Silberg WM, Lundberg GD and Mussachio RA (1997) Assessing, controlling and assuring the quality of medical information on the Internet. *BMJ* **277**:1244–5.
3 W3C, Platform for Privacy Preferences Project. *www.w3.org/P3P/ Overview.html*.

7 Other services

Introduction

Although the World Wide Web attracts the media's attention, and E-mail has become a standard method of communication, it is often forgotten that there are several other services available to the Internet user. These services may not attract the attention as easily as the Web, but they all offer particular benefits to the Internet user. Many of these services can now be accessed via your web browser, giving you access through one software package, but the software designed to be used with each service tends to offer better facilities than the compromised access provided by a web browser.

Newsgroups

Newsgroups allow people with a common interest to share their information and opinions within a forum. It works in a similar way to E-mail, where you compose messages and send them to an address. Where newsgroups differ from E-mail is that the address you send to is not to an individual, but the address of the forum or group.

To join a newsgroup, you need a software package, called a newsgroup reader, and the address of a newsgroup server. Most ISPs will provide a newsgroup service that provides access to the multitude of newsgroups, currently over 20 000, available on the Internet. Some ISPs will restrict the number of newsgroups available from their newsgroup server, and some also offer their own newsgroups for their subscribers. CompuServe is a good example of this, as it offers its own forums or communities, based on professional groupings such as medical, legal, and accountancy, in addition to the Internet newsgroups.

Various free newsgroup reader packages are available on the Internet, including Free Agent. Both Netscape Navigator and Internet Explorer offer limited newsgroup functionality, with Navigator having it built into the browser whereas Internet Explorer needs an additional piece of software that also provides access to E-mail, called Internet News and Mail.

Once you have access to a newsgroup, and have a newsgroup reader package, you can download the list of available newsgroups. This will take quite a while initially as you will need to download the full list; however, subsequent amendments to the list will be performed incrementally and will therefore be relatively quick.

The names of newsgroups are, like most of the Internet, structured in a logical manner to make it easier to identify groups that may be of interest. A guide to some of the most common codes is shown in the table below.

alt	Alternative groups, originally these were non-establishment sites offering alternative, anarchic, or outspoken forums. However, it is now one of the most popular categories, with some sites being more alternative than others
comp	Computer-related groups, ranging from good information sources to new users to technical sites for computer professionals
rec	Recreational subjects, covering a wide variety of hobbies and sports, for example rec.cycling
sci	Science-related topics, including medical groups
soc	Groups dealing with social issues
uk	Sites relating to UK issues, or providing a UK-based forum for the discussion of wider issues. There are further subgroupings within the UK (and other nationalities) heading, covering regions of the UK; for example, uk.regional.north-west

Using newsgroups

Once you have found the newsgroups that appear to share your interest you can subscribe to them. Once subscribed you can download the messages sent to the group, and join in the discussion 'threads' of the group. The term 'thread' refers to the string of postings that arise from an initial message sent to the group. A popular topic can give rise to many replies, and many responses to the replies, etc. To make this dialogue easier to follow, your newsgroup reader package will group together the messages sent about a particular subject into a 'thread'.

When you join a group, it is advisable to 'lurk' for an initial period, to gain an understanding of the topics being discussed within the group. 'Lurking' is the term used to describe someone who subscribes to a group without joining in the discussion, i.e. they read messages without writing back to the group.

To help you understand what is acceptable within the newsgroup, and the background of the group, there is usually a FAQ (frequently asked question) document that is designed to answer the questions of a newcomer to the group. This not only helps you to discover whether the group meets your needs, or interests, but also helps you to avoid inadvertently offending other members of the group, i.e. breaching the 'netiquette' of the group. Whenever joining a new group, it is advisable to be cautious, as the newsgroup community is notorious for its sensitivity to breaches in netiquette, and its propensity for flaming offenders. This reactionary nature has been moderated in recent years due to the large number of inexperienced users who have joined the Internet community, but it is still more prevalent in newsgroups than in any other Internet service.

A good place for new users of newsgroups to start is the *news.announce.newusers* or *news.newusers.questions* groups that are specifically designed for new users, answering many of the common questions that arise, and being more forgiving of a beginner's mistakes.

The number of messages exchanged within the group varies from group to group, with some generating very few messages while others produce a daily deluge of messages. To help users cope with the large number of postings that a group can generate, the more sophisticated newsgroup reader packages will allow you to view the titles of messages and threads without downloading the complete message. If you want to read a particular message, the reader will then download the message. This considerably reduces the amount of time you need to be connected to the news server.

For the medical researcher, there are a number of groups that may be of interest. These cover specific topics or more general areas of medicine or research. They include:

- *misc.education.medical*
- *medlux.medic.inform*
- *sci.med.informatics*
- *uk.sci.med.pharmacy*
- *uk.sci.med.ruralhealth*

Mailing lists

Mailing lists allow you to join in a newsgroup-style forum through your E-mail package. They work in the same manner as a newsgroup, where your messages are not posted to an individual but to a group. However, with a mailing list the message is sent to a central source, which then forwards the message to all the E-mail addresses within the group. In effect, you are sending an E-mail to a large number of people rather than sending a message to a central source that allows anyone else access to your message.

Mailing lists use an automated E-mail system to receive and forward mailings to users who have joined specified groups. Because of this, the syntax of messages sent to the system is very important. There are two major systems used to provide mailing lists, Listserv and Majordomo. The syntax of the two systems is slightly different, and a list of common commands is shown in the table below.

Join <mailing list> <name>	Join a mailing list, your name is normally added to the request to help identify you to other users, e.g. Join statistics John Smith
Leave <mailing list>	Stop receiving E-mail from the list, e.g. Leave medical-informatics
Suspend mail <mailing list>	Temporarily stop receiving E-mail from the list
Resume mail <mailing list>	Ends the period of suspension
Stop	Added at the end of a request to show that the commands have ended. Otherwise the system will try and interpret your E-mail signature, etc.

One of the major mailing lists, which will be of particular interest to British Internet users, is the mailbase system (*www.mailbase.ac.uk*). This system is based at Newcastle University and is aimed primarily at the British higher education community. However, there are a number of groups within it that will appeal to those involved in the healthcare sector. These include:

- admin-medical
- lis-medical
- medical-education.

A list of available mailing lists can be accessed via the Web at *www.liszt.com* and this site also provides a searchable listing of newsgroups.

Discussion forums

Another variation on the newsgroup theme is the web-based discussion forum that is incorporated into a specific web site. These are provided to allow visitors to a web site to air their opinions on topics covered by the site. They are becoming increasingly popular with web site designers as the discussion forum encourages visitors to return frequently to their site.

Discussion forums will normally have a starting topic and a web page-based feedback form, which you complete and then post to the web site. Your response will then appear on the web site, for visitors to read and respond to.

FTP

The file transfer protocol is used by most Internet users without realising they are using it. The FTP protocol is designed for the quick exchange of files between the user's computer and the FTP server on the Internet. It is often used when downloading files from the web as it is quicker and more efficient than using the native HTTP format of the web.

The major feature of the FTP protocol is that it is designed for transferring files not only from the Internet but also onto the Internet. For this reason, most web sites and other Internet content are posted onto the Internet using FTP, where the HTML pages are transferred to the web server via FTP.

Using FTP can be quite difficult as it is one of the older protocols, which relies heavily on the obscure command language of UNIX computer systems that is at the core of Internet protocols. There are a number of FTP packages available, the two most notable are WS-FTP and Cute FTP, which make the protocol more user-friendly.

When using FTP, you need to connect to an FTP server and then find the files you wish to download or the directory into which you want to upload files. To connect to an FTP server, you need to log into it using a user name and password; if you are accessing a restricted FTP server, you will need to obtain these from the administrators of the server. However, many FTP servers allow 'anonymous login', which uses your existing Internet user name and password to give you access to the public sections of the server. The public section of the FTP server is normally contained within a directory called 'pub' and an anonymous login will allow you to copy the files contained within this directory and its subdirectories. You would not normally be allowed to upload any files to the server.

Chat

The correct name for this Internet service is IRC (Internet relay chat) and, as the name suggests, it allows users to chat to one another. This normally takes place in discussion rooms or channels, where a number of Internet users meet to talk to one another. When someone types a message into their computer it is simultaneously transmitted over the Internet and almost instantaneously appears on the other users' screens. This allows the people within the room to maintain a dialog, rather than the stilted conversation via the sending and receiving of messages associated with E-mail, etc.

To use chat, you need to connect to an IRC server that acts as the focal point of the current chat channels. To connect to one of these servers you will need the IRC client software, although as with most other services you can use your web browser for many chat services. When you connect to the server you will need to log into the server, and provide your E-mail address and a nickname or alias that you will use in the chat rooms. Your nickname cannot be the same as any other user's, so most chat services will either ask you for an alternative nickname or validate it before letting you log into the service. Apart from this, your alias can be as serious or as irreverent as you wish and can be used to give an indication of your personality or hobbies.

Once signed into the IRC server you will be provided with a list of current chat channels and the number of people in it. You can enter any of the listed channels, but as with newsgroups it is advisable to join a group aimed at new users when first joining a chat service. These services are normally labelled 'beginners', 'irchelp', or 'newbies' to show they are for new users. Once you have joined a group, it is probably better to lurk until you have picked up the conversation and have something to add to the discussion; however, most channels will not frown on someone who joins the group with a 'Hi everyone, how's it going?' or similar message.

CompuServe and America Online (AOL) provide their users with their own chat rooms and these work in a similar manner to the Internet IRC channels. These are one of the most popular facilities offered by both providers and therefore both boast a good variety of chat rooms and discussion topics.

Chat allows people to have discussions with other chat users anywhere in the world, and this has received intermittent media attention due to the long-distance romances that have occurred via chat.

Another benefit of chat espoused by devotees includes the ability to conceal your identity or to assume an alter ego as the other chat users have no visual clues to your identity. An extension of this is where some chat services allow you to choose a computer-generated mannequin or avatar as a persona to use within chat sessions, allowing you to interact with other users both verbally and visually.

Gopher

The gopher service was once heralded as the future of the Internet, as it made the complex task of finding information on the Internet much easier for the user. Unfortunately for the gopher system, the World Wide Web was invented and it did all that gopher promised and more. This has led to the virtual demise of the gopher system, although there are a few sites remaining, mainly in the academic sector.

The gopher system, or 'gopher space', works by organising gopher servers (the equivalent of the WWW's web server) into various directories and subdirectories, in the same manner as a web-based directory listing. To find a gopher site, you would need to navigate through the relevant directories until you came to the documents and computer files held on the gopher server. This is quite easy to do, but lacks the multimedia effects of the Web and is also not as intuitive. This lack of intuitive links is probably the prime reason why gopher has been superseded by the Web.

Telnet

Telnet is another service that has been superseded by the presentation capabilities of the Web, with most telnet services moving to a web-based system.

Telnet allows the user to have remote control of a distant computer via an Internet link. This means you can conduct work on a much more powerful computer than your own personal computer, or a large number of people can undertake tasks simultaneously on a central computer.

The presentation of a telnet system will depend on the computer that you control remotely. It will tend to range from a basic text display that betrays the antiquated computer equipment that you are controlling, to graphic systems that resemble basic web pages. The content of a telnet system tends to be a large database of information, which you can search through, based on criteria you select. For example, the Medline database of journals used to be available via telnet to subscribers. However, one of the problems with telnet is that the commands used to control a session on the telnet computer vary from system to system, ranging from easy-to-follow menu systems to very basic systems with few clues to the commands used to operate the system.

Good examples of telnet include the BIDS system, which allows you to search the central store of information in Bath from your computer anywhere in the world. It is also a good example of how telnet systems have been transferred to the Web, as the BIDS system can now be accessed via the Web at *www.bids.ac.uk* rather than through the old telnet system.

Archie

Although FTP is a great method of obtaining various computer files from different computer systems, it is often very difficult to find the files you want to download. To help you find the files you want to obtain from an FTP server, there are various archi(v)e servers which maintain lists of files contained upon the various FTP servers connected to the Internet. The Archie system allows you to search these lists of FTP files in the same manner as a search engine is used to find web pages. You simply need to tell your Archie program the name of the file you are looking for, or part of the name, and point it to your favoured Archie server. The Archie program will attempt to find this file, and will display the location of the files that match your search criteria.

Finger/Ping

Finger and Ping are two very basic utilities that date back to the beginning of the TCP/IP protocol. These two facilities are very rarely used by anyone other than Internet technicians, but you may come across them while using the Internet.

The Finger utility can be used to gain information from another Internet user, when you know their user name and the domain address of their Internet-connected computer. This is rarely used nowadays, but some people still offer automated responses based on the address you finger, e.g. *support@computer.com* could provide a list of FAQs about the company's software package, whereas *newproducts@computer.com* would send you the latest information about the latest software packages.

The Ping utility is probably the simplest tool available, as it simply finds out if you can reach the address that you have specified. When you ping an address, your computer sends out a short message to the target computer and waits to see if the distant computer replies. This allows the Internet technician to check whether the destination computer is connected to the Internet, or whether it is unavailable. A practical application for this would be to see whether you could ping your ISP's computer when you are having difficulties connecting to the Internet. As a ping message is very small and simple, it may be able to reach your ISPs computer when larger, more complex information (such as a web page) is unable to be transferred. However, to use the Ping utility it is necessary to know the IP address of your ISP's computer, and any other computer you wish to ping, which requires some understanding of the technical aspects of TCP/IP.

8 Internet service providers

Introduction

The Internet is designed for use by computers that are permanently interconnected. This was not a problem in the early days of the Internet, when only universities and research organisations were attached to the Internet, as they could easily justify the resources required for a permanent connection, mainly by utilising these links for other purposes. However, for the average user and smaller organisations the benefits available from the Internet would be outweighed by the huge cost of maintaining this permanent connection.

To overcome this, companies called Internet service providers (ISPs) have been formed. These organisations maintain permanent connections to the Internet, and then sell small portions of this connection to individual users or organisations. This spreads the cost of the connection over a large number of users, making it economical for an individual to have their own connection. In real terms the simplest type of connection can be had for as little as £10 per month. It is even possible to gain free access; however, free access providers normally recover the costs of providing the service through other methods, such as premium-rate technical support telephone numbers.

The ISP will provide you with access to the Internet, but to use this you must connect to your ISP. The basic requirement for an individual is a modem for your computer and a telephone line, whereas most large organisations will use computer network equipment and a permanent connection to provide a faster connection for a wide range of staff to share. However, to make the most of the Internet, and especially the Web, some thought should be given to the specification of the computer used. A guide to the equipment needed to improve your use of the Internet is provided in this chapter.

There has been a wide proliferation of ISPs, ranging from small, regional companies to large, multinational organisations. These include specialist computer companies including IBM to high street stores and supermarkets, with Tesco offering Internet connections to its customers. The number of services offered by these organisations has also expanded as the Internet itself has expanded. This can make it very confusing for the new user to discern what facilities they need, and which ISP offers these facilities.

Computer equipment

One of the key features of the Internet is its open standards that allow different computer systems to communicate. This means there is a wide variety of computer systems available which are capable of connecting to the Internet, ranging from small 'personal digital assistants' (PDAs) such as the Psion 5, to the large UNIX systems which are the mainstay of the Internet's infrastructure. There are also a number of other devices, such as Web TV, that enable you to access the Internet via your TV and telephones.

However, although such devices as Web TV may make the Internet more accessible to the home user, in the business environment the main method of access will remain the personal computer. This section will refer to PCs running Microsoft Windows 95 or 98 directly, but most of the recommendations and comments will also apply to Microsoft Windows 3.1x or NT and Apple personal computers.

It is possible to use the Internet with a relatively old computer, as the remote computer undertakes much of the work when using E-mail, newsgroups, or FTP. However, if you use the World Wide Web regularly, an older computer will perform noticeably slower than a more modern PC. This will result in pages taking longer to fully download into your browser, more interrupted connections, and the inability to view web pages that utilise the latest features.

To make the most of Web browsing, or to improve your current computer's performance, you should look at a number of areas – the memory (often referred to as RAM), the graphics card/monitor, and the hard-disk size.

When you open a web page in your browser, the page and all its contents are copied from the web server into your computer's memory before being displayed. If your computer does not have enough memory to hold the complete page, it will move some of the page onto your hard disk. This slows performance, as your computer can read and write information more quickly to memory than to the hard disk. Therefore, by ensuring your PC has enough memory to cope with complete web pages, the time taken to retrieve web pages will decrease significantly. A common sign of too little memory is when you can hear your hard disk working when downloading a web page. In a Windows 98 PC the minimum recommended memory would be 32 Mb, with 64 Mb preferred.

One of the major advantages of the Web over the other Internet protocols is that it is a graphical environment, i.e. it uses pictures and colour as well as text. To make the most of this you need to have a good-quality graphics card and monitor. Most desktop PCs now come with a monitor that has a 15″ screen, with some better specification PCs having 17″ screens. A large number of monitors are also available separately, ranging in size from 14″ to 24″. The choice of monitor will depend on the software you use, the amount of room available, and personal preference. In general, a larger monitor is preferable when graphics software is used. The graphics card (sometimes referred to as a video card) is responsible for producing the images displayed on your monitor's screen. The choice of graphics card is linked to the size and quality of the monitor, with larger monitors needing better graphics cards.

The size of your computer's hard disk can also improve web browsing, as a larger hard disk allows you to increase the size of your browser's cache. The cache is a space on your computer's hard disk where visited web pages are stored for quick retrieval. With a larger cache, more web pages can be stored, resulting in less time spent downloading frequently visited pages. Also, frequent web browsers tend to find that their computer's hard disk is quickly filled with files and programs downloaded from the Web or E-mailed as attachments. With the increasing size of files available on the Web, the need for a larger hard disk will become increasingly noticeable.

Modems

If you are using the Internet frequently, you will want to use as fast a modem as possible. The faster your modem, the less time spent downloading web pages, sending E-mail, etc. which results in lower phone bills. The extra cost of purchasing a faster modem should be recouped in lower phone charges.

The most important feature of any modem is the baud rate at which it operates. This is the speed at which the modem transfers data over a telephone line. The baud rate can also sometimes be expressed as bps, which stands for bytes per second. The bps is also sometimes referred to as Kbps, which stands for kilobytes per second; this is the bps value divided by 1000. Most modems bought today will be rated as 56 600–baud or 56.6 Kbps, with a few older 33.6 Kbps modems still available. There are also a large number of 28 800–baud or 28.8 Kbps modems still in circulation, with some modems with lower baud ratings than this (e.g. 14 400–baud or 9600–baud) still in use. To add more confusion to the speed rating of modems, some manufacturers refer to the ITU (International Telecommunication Union) standard rather than the baud rating, where a V.90 modem and a V.32 modem perform at 56.6 Kbps and 28.8 Kbps, respectively. It should also be noted that the baud rate normally refers to the speed that the modem can send and receive information, but a 56.6 Kbps modem will only receive at this speed and will send at a maximum of approximately 33.6 Kbps. This is due to the limitations of telephone lines and the equipment at telephone exchanges.

The other option that might affect your decision when buying a modem is whether you want an internal or external style. An internal modem is fitted inside your PC's case, with the phone line connection at the back of the case. An external modem is contained within its own casing and is connected to your PC via the serial port. An external modem is easier to install and also has lights on the front to show what it is doing, but an internal modem is neater and only requires a telephone lead, compared to the mains, telephone, and serial cables required by an external modem.

There are a number of options available that allow you to obtain faster speeds than the 56.6 Kbps maximum of a modem. These range from ISDN, to direct cable connections, to satellite links. Unless there is a good reason to have a permanent connection to the Internet, the only real alternative to the modem is an ISDN connection. ISDN is a digital telephone line with two cables that can run at 64 Kbps each or be combined for 128 Kbps. The ISDN equivalent of a modem is called a terminal adaptor (TA) – this allows a PC to use an ISDN line instead of a telephone line. If you want to share Internet access between a number of networked computers (e.g. in a small office) an ISDN router can be used. An ISDN connection can be purchased from BT or any other telephone company.

Difference between ISP and OSP

Before the Internet made its leap from obscurity, there were already a number of organisations providing E-mail and information services via a modem connection to their computer network. These were referred to as on-line services, with the main service in the UK being CompuServe, which allowed its members to E-mail each other, look up information about various subjects, and take part in E-mail discussion groups.

The main difference between CompuServe and the Internet was that CompuServe's services and information were only available to its members whereas the Internet has always been accessible to all. CompuServe maintained this member-only status by controlling the computer network and the information contained within the network, which contrasts with anarchic interlinking of disparate systems that characterises the Internet.

As the Internet has become the global standard for computer communication, CompuServe and its ilk have adapted their proprietary systems to link with the Internet. However, they have retained their own computer networks with their member-only services. Therefore, to show this distinction, these organisations are often referred to as OSPs (online service providers). The three main OSPs are CompuServe, America Online (AOL), and the Microsoft Network.

These three organisations offer their members full access to the Internet for E-mail and web browsing, and supplement this with further information and services for their members only. The extra services offered vary between providers, with CompuServe aiming at professional people and their organisations, whereas America Online (AOL) and Microsoft Network (MSN) tread the middle ground, aiming for a mixture of work and home audiences. These extra facilities are often referred to as value-added services, and some industry commentators believe that more ISPs will offer these types of services to help differentiate them from the competition, whereas others believe that the OSPs will have to become more like the ISP providers, acting as a conduit for Internet access and leaving the provision of software and content to third parties.

The drawbacks of accessing the Internet via an OSP include additional charges and problems with proprietary standards. The OSPs all charge their members for the time spent connected to their network in addition to a monthly standing charge, compared to the flat fee offered by most ISPs. The other problem with OSPs will gradually diminish as they become fully-fledged Internet providers, but the occasional problem still occurs as they have adapted their proprietary systems to communicate over the Internet rather than using the Internet standards such as SMTP for mail, etc.

What to look for in a service provider

Due to the wide variety of providers offering Internet access, it can be difficult for the new user to discern which service is most suited to their needs. The two main areas to investigate with any provider are the cost and the services offered.

The cost of an Internet connection can vary dramatically between providers, and the structure of their charges can also make a substantial difference. The charges made vary from a flat fee for unlimited access to other services, which operate in the same manner as telephone companies with a fixed standing rate and an additional charge based on the time spent connected. The ISPs tend to operate the flat-fee system, with OSPs making charges for time spent connected. Another hidden extra with some companies is an initial one-off connection fee or a charge for the software used to access the provider's system. The other cost implication with an Internet connection is the telephone charges. To minimise these it is advisable to ensure that the provider has a telephone number that will be charged at the local call rate for your area. This can either be one of the national, local-call rate area codes (such as 0345 or 0845) or it can be through a network of local telephone numbers that includes your area. Another consideration for those who intend to use their connection while travelling the world should be the availability of international access numbers, as most ISPs are UK only or provide limited international access. This is one area where CompuServe excels, offering access from a large number of countries including western Europe and North America.

Although cost is the most obvious method of selecting a provider, it is advisable to check what services are provided for your money. Some ISPs do not support the full range of Internet protocols, omitting the less popular services such as gopher, FTP, and IRC. It is also possible to have a Web-only service or just an E-mail account. This can be cheaper than having the full range of services but can result in frustration if the information you seek can only be obtained using one of the protocols that is unavailable to you.

Perhaps one of the most important features of the service provided by an ISP that is often overlooked is the level of technical support provided. The Internet has become much more user friendly in the past few years, but it is still based on the complex networking and structure of TCP/IP. Therefore, there is more likelihood of problems occurring, as there are more potential trouble areas due to the links to the network. This is further exacerbated by the frequent updates to existing Internet software and the rapid development of new technology for use on the Internet. Due to this you are more likely to use the technical support services offered by your ISP than that offered for most of the other software installed on your computer system. Although it is very difficult to check the quality of technical advice given by an ISP before signing up to their service, there are a few indicators of the emphasis that the ISP gives to supporting its users. These include the opening hours of the technical support telephone lines and also whether they are charged at local or national rates. This is especially important if you know that you will be browsing the Web, etc. outside of office hours, as it is infuriating to have a problem at 8 p.m. and know that no one will be able to help you until after 9 a.m. the next day.

Other areas that are worth considering include checking the capacity or bandwidth of the Provider's connection to the Internet. The number of users will affect this, as 1000 users can comfortably share less bandwidth than 10 000. Therefore it is worth checking the ratio of users to bandwidth, and ensuring that the ISP has enough spare bandwidth to cope with peak periods. The effect of having a high number of users for the available bandwidth will result in more frequent lost connections, slower download speeds, and the inability to connect at peak periods.

A final consideration when selecting an ISP is the amount of storage space provided for your web pages. Most ISPs now offer a limited amount of space for each subscriber to display their web pages on the World Wide Web. The amount of space typically provided varies from as little as 2 Mb to as much as 15 Mb. The amount of space required for your web site will depend upon the content of your web site. A simple site consisting mainly of text and a few graphics could probably manage up to 50 pages in the 2 Mb minimum. However, if you intend to allow documents or files to be downloaded, or include Java applets or other more advanced features, then the 2 Mb could be quickly filled with a relatively small site easily consuming between 5 Mb and 10 Mb.

Software required

Another area in which the ISPs differ is the provision of software to access the protocols used on the Internet. All the different protocols require different software packages to gain the benefit of their different features. Most ISPs and all the OSPs offer a suite of software packages to access the protocols that they offer, either integrated into one user interface or a variety of packages that can be used for each protocol. By supplying the software and incorporating an easily followed set-up routine, these providers have made it very easy for a new user to connect to the Internet and access the services provided by the ISP or OSP. This has obvious benefits for most users and has helped make the Internet more accessible to less technically aware computer users.

The disadvantage of this approach is that you can be tied into the ISPs suite of software, making it very difficult to use other products. For example, if you are a frequent user of FTP software and found a particular FTP client software that you preferred to that provided by your ISP, it could be very difficult to integrate your preferred FTP software with the other ISP provided packages. For most users this will not be a problem, but it is worth considering how easy it would be to use your own software, as most experienced Internet users have their own set of preferred software packages for the various protocols.

Site hosting

As mentioned previously, most ISPs provide their subscribers with a small amount of space on their web servers for users to display their own web pages. However, these sites are relatively small and are aimed at the individual and small business user. For a more sophisticated web site, many ISPs have a separate business section, and there are also some specialist commercial web site providers. These offer sites that allow an organisation to have a professional presence on the Web rather than the small-scale personal web sites typically provided by consumer-orientated ISPs. This service is normally called web site hosting, as the commercial organisation stores your web site on their Internet-linked computer system.

The difference between these commercial sites and the personal web sites include the use of your own domain name and a faster connection to the Internet and E-mail addresses using the domain name. The domain name is the name that appears in the URL of a visitor's web browser (e.g. Swansea University's domain name is *swan.ac.uk*). The hosting organisation can normally arrange the registration of your domain name and ensure that if any web browser requests your domain name that they are directed to your site on their computer system. The use of a domain name gives your site a more professional appearance and also makes your site easier to find when compared to the addresses provided as part of your ISP account. For example, a site using Demon Internet's free web space will have the URL of *http://www.<your name or identifier>.demon.net* and a Pipex dial account would have *http://dblspace.pipex.dial/<your name or identifier>* where *<your name or identifier>* indicates the unique identifier used for your account. The use of a free web-space site for an organisation's web site is obvious to the web user and portrays an organisation that is not committed to using the web or is not prepared to invest in utilising the Web. Therefore, to be taken seriously by web users, an organisation should register their own domain name.

The other benefit of a good web site host is a much faster connection to the Internet that will not slow down the transmission of information to your site's visitors. This has obvious benefits as slow download speeds are one of the main causes for web users not returning to a site, and also affect the perceived quality of your site and organisation. To have a commercial site hosted will typically cost from £100 to £200 per annum for a relatively small site (10 Mb to 20 Mb), with prices rising as the amount of space required increases.

Other services that need to be considered when selecting a site host are the provision of E-mail aliases, the CGI-BIN utilities provided, and the support for Microsoft FrontPage extensions. E-mail aliases allow you to use your domain name in E-mail addresses within your site and then have any E-mail sent to these addresses automatically forwarded to your personal E-mail address (or other E-mail addresses within your organisation). This reinforces the professional appearance of your site and also hides your true E-mail address from web site visitors and potential spammers. The number of E-mail aliases varies, so the importance of this feature and the number of aliases offered should be considered when selecting your site host. The CGI-BIN utilities provided by the host could also affect your choice, as these are the small programs that process forms and count the number of visitors to your site, etc. If you want to use these utilities within your site, and especially if you have used forms within your site to gain information from visitors, you will need to ensure that the facilities are in place to process this data. The support for Microsoft FrontPage extensions is also very important if you use the Microsoft FrontPage HTML editor for your web page content and have used some of the advanced features offered by this package. As FrontPage uses its own proprietary standards to implement some advanced procedures, it is necessary to have a site containing these extensions hosted on a system that can understand how they are to be processed. Some hosts charge an additional fee for providing support for FrontPage extensions, and this should be considered when comparing hosts.

9 Intranet

Explanation of Intranet

The Internet has become a universal standard for exchanging information between computers, allowing a computer in the UK to communicate quickly and easily with another computer anywhere in the world. E-mail has become an essential means of communication and the Web is regarded as one of the best ways of disseminating and gathering information. The obvious benefits of the Internet in communicating with external organisations were quickly recognised as also applicable to internal communications within an organisation. This has led to organisations developing their own internal Internets or 'Intranets'.

An Intranet uses Internet technology to produce a computerised information system for staff within an organisation. Instead of making information available to a worldwide audience by connecting to the Internet, an Intranet is kept separate and inaccessible from the outside world. An Intranet is an organisation-wide web rather than a World Wide Web.

As Figure 9.1 shows, Intranets have been quickly adopted by a large number of organisations in the past few years, with 46% of the organisations surveyed in September 1997 having already installed, or currently installing, an Intranet. An Intranet in this survey was defined as 'access to corporate information using a Web browser and Internet Protocol'.

The NHS has developed its own Intranet called NHSWeb. This offers internal information viewed using a web browser and also includes E-mail facilities. This chapter will cover this Intranet, in addition to more general information regarding Intranets.

What the Intranet has to offer

The rise of the Intranet within organisations has been rapid for a number of reasons. The ease of use of the Web, and the simplicity of finding information, makes the Web an ideal method of disseminating information throughout an organisation.

It is an ideal way of storing and organising reference material for

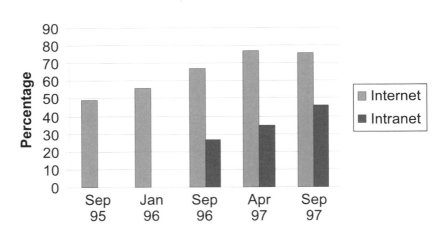

Figure 9.1 Percentage of surveyed organisations with Internet and Intranet installations. (From the Sixth Black Box Survey.)

staff to view as and when necessary, such as terms and conditions of service, or procedures for claiming travelling expenses, etc. An Intranet allows you to publish this information once in an easily found location, instead of issuing many paper copies that tend to be filed and forgotten. Fast-changing, dynamic information is also well suited to Intranet publication, because when the information is changed the most current version can be made available immediately via the Intranet, and the previous version automatically replaced. This means that anyone reading the page on the Intranet can be sure that it is the latest version.

The ability to ensure that the version viewed on the web page is the most current is due to the pages being stored in one central location – the web server. This centralised structure allows much tighter control of information and ensures that the displayed version of a document is the current standard.

Perhaps the reason why the uptake has been so rapid, rather than the steady growth normally associated with new technology, is that most organisations already have all the necessary equipment and software needed to establish an Intranet. Also, the two major network operating systems, Microsoft NT and Novell NetWare, both have a web server as part of their system, and any PC with Windows 95 onwards has a web browser pre-installed (i.e. Microsoft Internet Explorer). Further, due to very competitive marketing, browser software is available for free from both of the major vendors.

Therefore, for most organisations, an Intranet can be established quickly without high equipment or software costs.

The centralisation of information has made the Intranet attractive to IT departments as it has restored the control of the computer system to the IT department. Another reason for the popularity of Intranets with IT departments is that this centralisation also means that most of the computing power required to run an Intranet is at the web server. This allows older, less-powerful PCs to access the Intranet, without the need for costly upgrades or replacements.

Information that wouldn't appear on the Internet

Intranets have developed from the World Wide Web and the Internet with the aim of disseminating information using the same technology. However, due to the closed nature of an Intranet, the actual information contained within an Intranet can be quite different to that found on the Internet. Because the audience of an Intranet is restricted to within the organisation, it is possible to include information that is either too sensitive for the public domain or only of interest to people within the organisation.

This allows Intranets to contain information regarding personnel policies, or details of sales promotions, etc. without the risk of outside organisations seeing the details. The security of an Intranet allows the quick dissemination of sensitive information without the fear of this information being inadvertently leaked.

Intranets can contain information that is especially targeted at the audience, and offer specialist services to this audience. As the users of an Intranet are known, unlike the anonymity and universal nature of the World Wide Web, it is possible to publish information that is only relevant to this audience or a small subset of this audience. A good example of this on the NHS Intranets is the number of Trusts who publish their policies and procedures, which are only relevant to the Trust's own staff and perhaps of interest to other Trusts' policy committees.

E-mail on the Intranet

An important component of the NHS Intranets is the provision of E-mail to users of the Intranet, as it provides a valuable means of communication of medical information and other data between

NHS staff. The connection of most NHS bodies to the E-mail system is seen as strategically important to the modernisation of NHS communications. One of the main reasons for launching a national initiative to achieve this goal is the idea that by connecting senior executives and encouraging them to communicate via E-mail they will support the development of the NHSNet and other IM&T projects.[1] This will help reduce the cost of NHS communication due to the low cost of E-mail in comparison to the traditional postal and courier methods.

The E-mail systems used on the NHS Intranet differ from those used by individual Internet users, as the software is more powerful and the protocol used to exchange messages is also more flexible than that used on the Internet. The E-mail software used on NHSNet is limited to three packages that not only offer E-mail but a variety of organiser utilities, such as diaries and appointment schedulers. These three packages are Lotus CC: Mail, Microsoft Exchange and Novell GroupWise. The actual package used is decided within the organisation, but Intranet E-mail co-ordinators do promote a particular package in an attempt to provide a standard platform across their respective areas. These packages offer a variety of features not supported by the simple mail transfer protocol (SMTP) used by E-mail on the Internet, including the formatting of text and other enhancements. As each package has its own proprietary standards, a common protocol is required to allow communication between sites using different E-mail packages. The standard used throughout the NHS Intranet is not the Internet standard of SMTP but another protocol called X.400. This has several advantages over the SMTP standard of the Internet, the primary improvement being increased security. This helps to maintain the privacy and confidentiality of information exchanged between sites. However, there is still an obvious need to allow communication with people outside the NHS who use the Internet for E-mail. To facilitate this, a number of Internet 'gateways' are installed, which act as intermediaries between the NHS Intranet and the Internet, allowing E-mail to pass between Internet and Intranet users.

One of the most useful features of the Intranet's X.400-based system is the ability to maintain an address book of all E-mail users connected to the Intranet. This allows users to find the address of anyone who has an Intranet E-mail address quickly and easily, easing communication between NHS employees. However, these address books have to be maintained separately by each E-mail system connected to the Intranet. This requires a high level of co-ordination and co-operation between the various sites on the Intranet, although much of the work is performed automatically by the newer versions of the E-mail systems. To overcome this need for each site to maintain its own address book, the NHS Intranets are developing a method of maintaining one central store of E-mail addresses that can be accessed by all sites. This has obvious benefits, including the reduction in time spent maintaining the separate lists and the increased accuracy of one central list instead of a multitude of duplicate address books. However, the X.400 standard does not support this centrally stored and administered address book, as this feature can only be implemented using the X.500 protocol.

Limiting Internet access

The NHS Intranet gives users access to the Internet, allowing users to link seamlessly from an Intranet site to a site on the World Wide Web. This initially appears an oxymoron as an Intranet is a closed version of the Internet, therefore by allowing Internet access the closed system is made open. However, the access to the Internet is restricted by a firewall. The firewall sits in the no-man's land or 'DMZ' (demilitarised zone) between the Internet and the local computer network that comprises the Intranet. Its job is to check the traffic between the local network and the Internet, checking where on the Internet a local computer is trying to reach, and what computers on the Internet are trying to gain access to the local network.

This allows the administrators of the NHSNets to monitor the World Wide Web pages being requested by Intranet users, and to exclude certain sites from being accessed. Another feature of some firewalls is the ability to virus check incoming web pages or E-mail.

Code of connection

To ensure the security of the Intranet, it needs to be protected from external threats. For a simple Intranet within a single organisation this will probably be tied in with the existing computer network security, such as user names and passwords and the implementation of a firewall. However, the NHS Intranets are more complex and require special measures, as weak security at one site could impact on another organisation's computer systems. To ensure that all organisations that connect to the Intranet have adequate security controls, they must implement a security policy that meets or exceeds the standards outlined in the code of connection. This code of connection includes minimum specifications for areas such as passwords and antivirus protection. It also prohibits connections to other networks, including the Internet and JANET. It is based on best practice within the IT and telecommunication security fields, and tries to lay out in simple terms the security requirements of connecting to the network for different types of NHS organisation and connection.[2]

The NHSNet offers six types of connection (listed below), covering the spectrum of NHS organisations and the level of connection required.

- Full-service access – a permanent connection to the NHSNet, providing the highest level of service available. It also includes limited access to the Internet.
- Dial-up service – where a permanent connection is not justified, a dial-up connection via a modem or ISDN can be arranged, in the same manner as for the Internet connection described in Chapter 8. As this type of connection is more vulnerable, a 'strong authentication' method of user verification is required. An example of this is the Secure ID system that uses a small, pager-type device to produce a code that is updated every few minutes. To connect to the network you must enter the correct current code as part of the logging-in procedure.
- Messaging only – this service provides the benefit of an E-mail connection without the additional Intranet facility.
- General practice service – specifically designed for the needs of GPs and offering services tailored to their requirements.
- Security transition – an interim agreement can be arranged for organisations that do not currently meet the requirements of the full agreement. Limited access can be provided while they overcome the deficiencies in their security procedures.
- Third-party access – for non–NHS organisations who have a valid reason for connecting to the NHSNet. This agreement needs to be sponsored by an NHS organisation and includes a non-disclosure of NHS information clause.[2]

There is also a code of practice that all connected organisations must abide by, which ensures the accuracy and legality of the information displayed upon the NHS Intranets. The rules included in the code of practice include measures such as ensuring that the material has 'a positive endorsement from an appropriate professional body' and that the material does not bring 'discredit upon or reduce confidence in the NHS or the Department of Health'.[3] These aim to ensure that users of the Intranet can be confident of the validity of information displayed, in contrast to the large amount of dubious and unsubstantiated information available on the Web.

These codes are designed to ensure that any NHS organisation connecting to the Intranet has a minimum standard of security in place to help prevent unauthorised access to sensitive NHS information, and that the information posted is accurate and timely. It does not provide absolute security, as this is impossible to guarantee and would be too cumbersome to achieve. Therefore, it is possible for an organisation to extend their security policies beyond the standards included in the code, but not to implement security that does not meet the guidelines.

Extranets

As Intranets have spread through most organisations it has become increasingly apparent to many of these organisations that the benefits of their Intranet could also benefit their relationships with suppliers and other partner organisations. This has led to some organisations extending their Intranet or parts of it, to other bodies they co-operate with. These Intranets with links to external organisations are commonly termed Extranets. This term could be used to describe the NHS Intranets, as they are a number of separate Intranets run by Trusts and health authorities which link together to share information, while restricting access to certain information (such as personnel policies and internal announcements) to users within the organisation.

Another way in which the security and control mechanisms of an Intranet can be extended to other bodies outside an organisation is via a virtual private network (VPN). This uses the Internet as a communication medium while retaining privacy by encrypting the information during transmission over the public Internet network.

VPNs have become increasingly popular amongst organisations spread over a large geographical area.

The benefits of NHSWeb

NHSWeb is designed to provide benefits in the delivery of healthcare, communication and consultation, planning of healthcare and the development of healthcare strategies, programmes, and staff.[4]

These benefits will be derived from the improved access to information and the streamlining of information exchange between NHS bodies. The idea is to promote research-based best practice, based upon the information available on the Intranet and the wider resources of the Internet. This includes the publication of research on the Intranet alongside morbidity and epidemiology data, hazard notices, and health promotion literature. This will allow users to access quickly and easily relevant healthcare information and well-researched advice on best practice. The idea is to produce a snowball effect of research and best-practice policy information, leading and promoting other users to produce more information to create a knowledge base of well-researched and authenticated information for the benefit of healthcare practitioners.

The Intranets currently offer a number of services to help and promote this research. The services offered include:

- statistical databases
- training and educational material
- official communications, such as DGMs, hazard notices, CMO announcements, etc.
- knowledge bases, including Medline
- E-mail and newsgroups to help individuals communicate.

Ultimately, as more and more NHS organisations realise the benefits of the Intranet and E-mail, many communications between NHS bodies, such as discharge and test result information, will be disseminated quickly through the NHSNet links.

References

1   Editorial (1998) *Br J Hlthcare Comput Inform Manag* **15(1)**:2.
2   Yeomans R (1998) Connecting to NHSNet: the role of codes of connection. *Br J Hlthcare Comput Inform Manag* **15(1)**:27–30.

3   NHS Executive (1998) *NHSWeb Code of Practice*, IMG ref no. H8041. NHS Executive, Leeds.
4   NHS Executive (1998) *NHSNet: the Benefits for NHS organisations*, IMG ref no. H8030. NHS Executive, Leeds.

10 The Intranet as an organisational communications medium: a case study

Mike Ingham

Summary

Lincoln District Healthcare NHS Trust has established a web site on its Intranet. This chapter describes the identification of the business need, together with the information technology infrastructure which made the Intranet web site possible, and examines the factors affecting the acquisition, commissioning, and use of the facility.

The Trust

Background

Established in 1994, Lincoln District Healthcare NHS Trust provides an extensive range of community- and hospital-based health services across the city of Lincoln and the central part of Lincolnshire.

This area of the county is largely rural and covers almost 1000 square miles. Staff are based at more than 70 sites as well as GP practices, and there are 350 designated inpatient beds. In 1997 the Trust was awarded the Charter Mark.

The dispersed nature of the Trust presents a number of problems, and in particular those affecting the need for communications and data networking, which differs greatly from that of a single-site acute general hospital.

The place of IM&T

The role of IM&T within the Trust is to:

- develop and manage an effective information environment
- ensure the availability of information to
  - support the provision of effective healthcare
  - inform patients and the public

- enable the management of the trust and the efficient use of resources
- add value.

Much has been achieved over recent years with the establishment and development of a robust IT infrastructure in the Trust, which meets local and national needs, is controlled and secure, and has the ability to grow.

The Intranet web site project

Purpose

The Intranet web site was established to provide clinicians and managers with access via the Trust WAN to up-to-date reports on finance, quality, manpower, contracts, and patient activity, and to provide a gateway into the Internet. This met a clear business need.

The web site is complemented by, and complements, other initiatives in the fields of clinical and corporate governance, and in the development of the Trust communications policy and performance-monitoring structure.

The setting

The establishment of the Trust Intranet web site was in line with the Trust's corporate objectives[1] and IM&T development plan[2] as well as national initiatives.

The 1996 White Paper *A Service with Ambitions*[3] stressed the importance of the way the NHS uses information. This theme was developed further in the 1997 White Paper *The New NHS*,[4] which identified the development of web-based communications as an essential management and clinical tool. Guidance on Intranets has been issued.[5]

The 1998 NHS Information Strategy[6] notes the value of Intranets, the importance of exploiting the potential of the Internet, and the benefits of using Internet technology to present a consistent appearance to users. Research has been funded as part of the strategy in the use of information and communications technology in extending information to patients and the public.

The decision to establish the web site actually placed the Trust ahead of the 1997 White Paper and the 1998 NHS Information Strategy.

Content of the Trust Intranet

The Trust's intranet consists of the following components:

- Trust WAN
- WAN server
- Intranet web server
- NHSNet access
- E-mail
  - internal
  - NHS (X.400)
  - Internet (SMTP)
- faxes outward
- Internet/WWW access.

The business need

There is a need for information, covering many areas, to be available readily to directors, clinicians, and all those managing the Trust. This information should be easily accessible, and produced in a low-cost, low-resource manner.

Information systems must function within a management framework of an organisation, and the task of the Intranet web site project was thus management focused rather than simply systems focused.

The Intranet site as a solution

The existence of the IT infrastructure across the Trust, together with the appropriate network architecture, suitable PC platforms/software, and relevant IT skills made the introduction of an Intranet web site a practical initiative.

Commissioning the Intranet web site was outsourced to the network consultants who had provided the firewall hardware. The only additional skill required was that of web authoring, and the ability to produce an attractive layout and style built on presentational skills already in use in more traditional publications (Figure 10.1).

An understanding of the Internet and World Wide Web was necessary (but existing in the IM&T department, two staff having their own Internet home pages) as was the ability to produce text in HTML (hypertext markup language) – although for this suitable

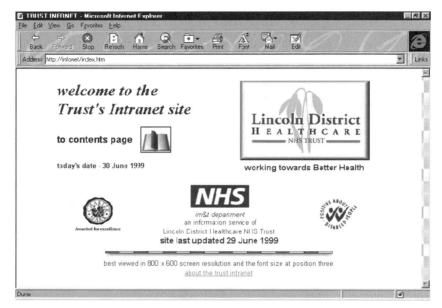

Figure10.1 Setting the style – the web site's home page.

tools are readily available to transform standard word-processed text into HTML format, as are suitable textbooks.[7]

Given the capability, this was an attractive, low-cost, low-risk project. Direct start-up costs were limited to a mid-range (at that time) PC which could have been redeployed if the project had failed, and modestly priced web site software. The total cost of the server, software, installation, and commissioning was £4275 (1997 prices).

How was this achieved?

- By using the IT infrastructure developed across the Trust.
- By using the flexibility and compatibility of the software standards adopted.
- By using existing technology to host a web site.
- By employing Internet browser technology to present a standard front end to users, and a seamless format to move from system to system (where possible the start/home page of each user's browser is set at the Trust Intranet web site home page).
- By presenting users with information in an easily accessible way, in a more readily understood form, and in a standardized format.

- By providing benefits to users, delivering new capabilities as well as solutions to existing information needs.
- By presenting information in one place, breaking from the established pattern of management information in a vertical stratification, and demonstrating the benefits of such amalgamation.

Content of the web site

What is provided?

Content (Figure 10.2) falls into six main groups:

- latest detail on Trust performance
- library of Trust policies/reference documents
- look-up directories
- software downloads
- latest/breaking news items
- links to Internet sites.

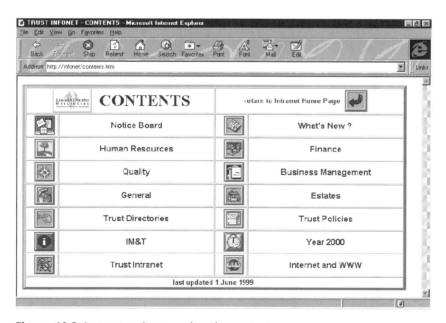

Figure 10.2 A structured approach – the contents page

What can be provided?

Essentially anything that can be converted into an HTML format (or GIF/JPEG for graphics) can be incorporated (Figure 10.3). The only limitation is the time involved in preparing and controlling the web site.

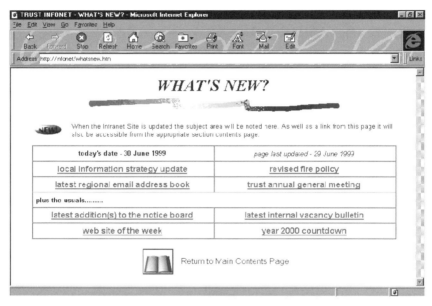

Figure 10.3 Keeping up to date – the 'What's new?' page.

Directorates have been encouraged to develop their own local style and content, with the IM&T department acting as 'publisher'. However, as part of the conversion into HTML there are checks for the overall house style and layout consistency, and potential conflicts with other sections and material.

Standard IT security controls are applied and it is possible to include a hierarchy of content if required, the web site software allowing structured access to different levels to be permitted to individual users.

Another key principle employed, to keep the workload within appropriate limits, is to carry out routine updates on a weekly basis. A result of this is the attraction of an ever-changing site, which helps to maintain interest.

What's in a name?

When the Intranet web site was established, it was decided to give it a name. After much debate 'Infonet' was chosen, reflecting its nature and purpose. Only a few months later a press release from the software developer Borland announced that it had coined the term 'Infonet' to describe a network of connected resources that co-operate to transform a corporation's data resources into realtime information that is customized for, and meaningful to, its users. The Trust's Intranet project team felt that it had been pretty close.

The technology

Establishment of the Trust WAN

Until the autumn of 1996 all major networking was provided by a district-wide network with a gateway to the regional network. This was used for terminal access to the main patient administration system and the community information system, which were based at the main acute hospital.

When the Trust headquarters (HQ) was established in the current building in 1991 a small local area network (LAN) was set up by the IM&T department. The HQ was cabled throughout at the end of 1994 and a new server commissioned in early 1995. This was a Compaq ProSignia 500, operating Novell NetWare.

A pilot to make management information available on the server began in May 1995, early trials with patient activity information proving a success. The intention, even at this early stage, was to extend the information available to include finance, manpower, and quality.

The district and regional networks were shut down in the late summer of 1996, each organization then linking into the NHS national network (NHSNet). The Trust had embarked on an ambitious programme to improve the reach of the Trust WAN and its capabilities. This included:

- reprovision of all Trust data links direct to the Trust HQ
- establishment of a dedicated link to NHSNet
- use of NHSNet for all external data communications
- provision of internal and external E-mail
- establishment of a firewall

- availability of access into the Internet.

By October all the targets had been met and the Intranet web site was commissioned in March 1997.

The current environment

All the main sites of the Trust have full network access on the Trust WAN, and other key sites have terminal access to the two main patient administration systems. An upgrade programme is in hand, which is extending full network access. NHSNet services are managed for another Trust and central computer and IT support services are provided from the IM&T department.

NHSNet is used by the Trust to access systems including finance, payroll, supplies, and patient administration which are run on a bureau basis at other locations. The Trust HQ link to the NHSNet allows additional capacity for growth, traffic reports indicating that only occasionally does the bandwidth usage exceed 55%.

Users with full network access are able to link into NHSNet-supported services, including the Internet. Services available include internal E-mail, NHS executive E-mail using the X.400 standard, Internet E-mail, and the ability to send faxes from PCs.

The WAN server is a Compaq ProLiant 5500, running under Microsoft Windows NT, and was commissioned in May 1998. The Intranet web site server is a P200 PC with a 2 Gb hard drive and 32 Mb RAM, operating the O'Reilly WebSite software under Windows 95. The working files are held on the WAN server and uploads to the Intranet server are made using a basic FTP freeware package.

Security has been a key factor, as evidenced by the firewall being operational from the time that the link was first made to NHSNet, and the Trust received full security classification under the NHS Executive Code of Connection.[8] This is an area that must be monitored continuously to ensure compliance with all relevant policies.

The PC environment of the Trust has been standardized on Microsoft products, using Windows 95. This gives users a familiar and standard environment, where new developments integrate seamlessly and additions are intuitive in nature keeping training implications to a minimum. The freely available Microsoft Internet Explorer web browser is an additional benefit, and there is the assurance that all content on the Trust web site will appear the same to all users.

Trust Intranet – the project

How has the project developed in practical terms?

As a project, the task has been undertaken using basic problem-solving techniques as well as a standard project management protocol[9] using PRINCE principles, within the Trust's existing IM&T projects management structure. An integrated approach was adopted, involving a number of managers.

Initially, the task was to prove that the concept worked – that the technology actually did what it was supposed to do, and that users could access the web site. It was accepted that some web authoring work would be required to set up the structure of the site and produce a standard house style. To reduce the workload it was planned that the initial content would comprise existing documents (for example, the telephone directory).

One unplanned benefit has been improvements in the presentation of some reports submitted to the Trust Board. The need for easy graphical presentation on the web site led to the adoption of a similar style on paper reports.

The project team comprises the author (acting as web master), network manager, systems administrator, plus representatives of the main directorates of the Trust, including the two clinical directorates. Although this may be regarded as being on the high side for numbers, it was essential that the key functions of the Trust would be represented, with the additional emphasis of the need for the support of clinical managers.

It was also decided to keep the technical development aspects somewhat separate from the web site content, although all involved were known to be enthusiastic about the use of IT, and approaches were only made to those who were expected to respond positively. To ensure support from senior management, the approval of relevant directors was sought before the actual approach was made to individuals.

The development of content has been a phased process, inserting new sections at intervals rather than attempting to have everything at once. This approach was adopted from the practical point of view (the size of the task also dictating that the project team would develop by sharing experiences) and to encourage the interest of users in an ever-changing site.

Factors involved

The key factors of the project can be summarized as:

- scope
- project management
- levels/range of access
- existing/available user skills
- training issues
- web site maintenance
- IT support
- security
- inappropriate use.

Why did it require an integrated approach?

The web site is not a stand-alone issue. To move such a project forward would have been impossible without the support of others, both the approval of the directors and the active involvement of those on the project team. It was ensured that key influencers had the web site capability from an early stage.

Although the author and IM&T staff could see the potential of this initiative – together with the very real benefits which could flow from it – they could not even hope to be successful without the application of a range of skills, the commitment and involvement of others, the IT infrastructure to support it, and an overall management culture which would encourage it.

Advantages of this approach

- Sharing of skills (local and external).
- Sharing of risk, workload, and cost.
- Commitment and joint ownership.
- Team-building process.
- A joint project, part of the overall management process of the Trust.

No real disadvantages were encountered or perceived.

People

Although the use of project management methodology gave a clear framework in which to work, the introduction of the Intranet web site forms part of the evolution of the Trust, so the project is a change management issue. More significantly, perhaps, it can be viewed as part of business process re-engineering by rethinking the use of systems and introducing a fundamental change in the empowerment of individuals accessing and using information, and by achieving improvements in the measurement of performance.

Above all, change is about people. Although change will be defined in terms of efficiency, effectiveness, meeting challenges, and taking opportunities, it has the implicit value of disrupting people's lives. This may be perceived as a threat, even if the need for change is accepted, and care was taken to recognise this important aspect.

Management styles

Management of the project used a mixture of three main management styles:

- logical − a direct approach, drawing attention to the benefits
- persuasive − delivering benefits and meeting user wants
- proactive − introducing improvements without being asked.

The intention was to provide something which was seen as useful by managers, gave them direct benefits, and which convinced them, almost without posing a question to them. It was a further step to meet the need for managers and staff at all levels to understand and use information.

Risks and benefits

Risks

- **Failure of technology** − the IT infrastructure is very robust, uses standard platforms, and the technology employed meets international standards; assessed as low risk.
- **Failure of project team** − the size of the team ensured a level of input redundancy, so individual members' workloads were not excessive, all are extremely competent in their own field and relate

well to each other in the informal style of project management that was adopted; assessed as low risk.

- **Lack of interest/commitment by the Trust Board** – despite the demonstrable benefits, it was possible that the web site might have been regarded as unnecessary; assessed as low to medium risk.
- **Loss of credibility of the IM&T function if the project failed to deliver** – the project has been seen to deliver and continues to be used; assessed as low risk.

Benefits

- A readily accessible and useful tool for managers.
- A foundation on which to develop management information.
- Extended use of existing IT at no additional cost.
- Good teamworking.
- Useful skills development for all the project team.
- Practical demonstration of value of IM&T to the organization.

Further extending staff communications, and also providing useful facilities.

The lessons learned

The issues involved

- Define the purpose and objectives.
- The need for proper project management.
- Support from the top.
- Presentational issues.
- Educational/technophobia issues.
- The need for (and use of) technically skilled people.
- Enthusiastic people on the project team.
- The value of trend setters/opinion formers.

What else?

- Define the need.
- Was this a solution looking for a problem?
- Just because we could do it, did it mean that we should?

Has it worked?

Overall – yes

One feature of the software is a reporting capability on usage of the web site, which shows mean weekday hits in a typical month of 250–300 per day, with a maximum of over 500 hits in one day. The peak period is 2 p.m. to 3 p.m. – early in the project it was 1 p.m. to 2 p.m., which suggests an acceptance of the service as a business tool rather than primarily for lunchtime surfing.

Technically – yes

- The existing technologies enabled an Intranet service to function.
- An Intranet web site server was commissioned with minimal effort.
- Users can access the site easily.
- Existing web-authoring skills were utilized.
- Updates are easily achieved.
- It has room to grow.

Process/project management – yes

- The process to deliver the project worked.
- The project achieved all the targets that were set.
- The team has worked extremely well together.
- New ideas have been generated.
- Working relationships have been strengthened.
- The team is keen to try more.

Managerially – yes

- The Intranet is used (unknowingly perhaps by some users).
- The web site is used.

but

- Not everyone recognises the benefits/capabilities.
- Not every manager has access to the web site yet.

115

The Trust Internet web site

As well as an Intranet site, the Trust also has a public Internet site. Although simple in design, a full web presence is desirable, and the experience gained on the Intranet project was put to good use.

The Trust's network could host an Internet web site server but the additional burden of support to a public site was not considered appropriate and a commercial Internet service provider was the most practical solution. A further step forward is anticipated through a proposed joint Lincolnshire health services Internet site using the *.nhs.uk* domain name.

Where next?

It will be appreciated that the project is still evolving, and further developments may be viewed from two perspectives.

- The practical, what feature is added next?
- The more organizational development aspect, of what needs to follow so as to ensure that the real needs of users are/will be met.

The first area is progressing well. An agreed development plan exists, and a list of further features is being implemented.

Improvements in presentation are being made (for example, the use of frames) and more adventurous items, such as the use of sound and animated graphics, but it is recognized that not every user has a high-specification PC and might not appreciate IT-intensive features. Perhaps a more ambitious development may follow consideration of introducing a browser front end for all users on booting up their PC. The developments introduced by Microsoft, integrating Windows 98 and Internet Explorer, are noted with interest.

The greater work is required in the second area. An ongoing task is to give access to the web site to more people within the Trust and to upgrade services to existing users. It is intended that those sites that cannot be hard-wired into the WAN will be given secure dial-in network access.

The Intranet could be developed to form an Extranet available to GPs and other local health organizations. This is in line with the NHS White Paper and the national Information Strategy. At the time of writing the Trust is one of those chosen to pilot a regional

Intranet site and further enhancements will also take place to the Trust's Internet web site.

Another development being considered is the use of interface software to feed information into the Intranet from disparate systems, rather than the manual translation currently in use, and so allow dynamic access to data across the Trust.

Whatever the detail or information provided, the overall purpose remains the same, and whenever there are clear benefits to the Trust and its services Internet technology will play a key role.

References

1 Lincoln District Healthcare NHS Trust (1996) *Business Plan 1996/ 1997*. Lincoln District Healthcare NHS Trust, Lincoln.
2 Ingham MJ (1996) *IM&T Developments: 1996/1997–1999/2000*. Lincoln District Healthcare NHS Trust, Lincoln.
3 Secretary of State for Health (1996) *The NHS: A Service with Ambitions*. Cmd 3425. The Stationery Office, London.
4 Secretary of State for Health (1997) *The New NHS, Modern – Dependable*. Cmd 3807. The Stationery Office, London.
5 Institute of Helath and Care Development (1998) *Introducing Intranets*. Institute of Health and Care Development, Bristol.
6 Burns F (1998) *Information for Health*. NHS Executive, Leeds.
7 Martin TA and Davis G (1997) *The Project Cool Guide to HTML*. J Wiley and Sons, New York.
8 NHS Executive (1995) *NHS-Wide Networking Programme*. NHS Executive, Leeds.
9 Ingham MJ (1997) *Trust Intranet Development: Project Initiation Document*. Lincoln District Healthcare NHS Trust, Lincoln.

11 Web-page design

Introduction

This chapter will demonstrate how to produce a basic web page that can be posted on the World Wide Web or the NHSNet. This will provide an insight into how web pages and web sites are constructed, and how the components of a web page operate.

It is beyond the scope of this chapter to provide extensive details of HTML authoring or web page design. However, the fundamentals will be covered in this chapter and further information and tutorials are available from a variety of sources on the Internet, and a number of publications are devoted to the subject.

What is HTML?

Nearly all web pages are written using HTML (hypertext markup language). HTML is designed to be a container for web page components, such as images or Java applets, and to provide links between HTML documents. The basic building block of the language is the tag, which is a piece of code that indicates the start of a component, with a similar tag denoting the end of the component. There are a wide variety of tags, with new ones under constant development to meet the needs of the constantly expanding content of web pages. All tags are enclosed in the <> style brackets, for example, the tag to denote italicised text is <I> with the closing tag of </I>.

Your web browser translates these tags and the contents of the tags are displayed. For example, when your browser finds the <B> tag it emboldens the following text until the </B> tag is reached. With the basic tags, like <B>, all browsers will translate this in the same manner. However, with more complex tags, each browser can translate the contents in subtly different ways. This can result in some web pages written in the 'universal' HTML format being displayed quite differently by different browser packages. Another common problem is that an older version of a browser is incapable of translating some of the more recent tags, resulting in the content of these tags being ignored.

The other major problem is that both Microsoft and Netscape (the two companies that dominate the browser market) include and promote new tags that are not officially included within the HTML standard. This results in some features only being available to users of one company's browser.

This disparity between the major browsers needs to be taken into account when designing web pages, as the users of a web site could be using either package. Some sites indicate the particular browser package that will give optimum performance with the site. Other, more sophisticated, sites duplicate their web pages, with one set of pages optimised for Internet Explorer, and the other optimised for Navigator. The site then automatically checks which browser you are using and guides you to the correct set of pages. Both these solutions are far from ideal, and most sites can be made to display correctly in both browsers by careful manipulation of the tags.

HTML editors

The number of HTML authoring software packages has grown considerably in the past few years, with all the major software companies offering a product. As with all Internet software, a number of good-quality packages can also be downloaded for free (for a trial period). The leading HTML authoring packages include Microsoft FrontPage, Adobe Pagemill and HoTMetaL Pro. Most modern word processors (and spreadsheets, desktop publishing packages, etc.) also allow you to save files in HTML format. Using these packages, you can quickly and easily produce web pages without seeing or directly using HTML tags. HTML can also be the core file format for Microsoft Office 2000, the main suite of software packages used with PCs.

However, unlike a word processor or spreadsheet, it is not necessary to purchase an HTML authoring package to produce HTML documents, as HTML is written in ASCII text format. Therefore a simple text editor, such as the Notepad program included with Microsoft Windows, can be used to create web pages.

To create the pages detailed in this chapter you can use the Notepad package or any other text editor, rather than a word processor or HTML authoring package.

HTML essentials

All HTML documents start with the <HTML> tag and end with a </HTML> tag. This allows any browser package (or any other HTML-aware software package) to identify the document as HTML. The HTML document consists of two parts, the header and the body sections of the document. These use the <TITLE> and <BODY> tags, respectively.

The title section contains all the information regarding the page, including the title. The contents of this section are not displayed within the browser's window.

The body section is where the web page content is entered. Any information that is to be displayed within the browser's window needs to be within this section.

This means that an HTML page must contain the following before any content is added:

```
<HTML>
<TITLE>
</TITLE>
<BODY>
</BODY>
</HTML>
```

Creating a simple web page

The easiest way to demonstrate the simplicity of HTML is to create a simple web page. The following section will show you how to create a simple text page, how to add hyperlinks, and also how to display graphics.

Step 1: simple text page

The following HTML code produces the web page shown in Figure 11.1. As you can see, the title of 'My First Web' page appears in the top bar of the browser (in this example Microsoft Internet Explorer) and also in large text as we have marked this as <H1> – a heading of the highest level (level 1). The text of the page is enclosed in the <P> tag that indicates a paragraph of text. The <BR> tag in the midst of the paragraph indicates a line break in the text.

Figure 11.1 A simple web page.

```
<HTML>
<HEAD>
<TITLE>My First Web Page</TITLE>
</HEAD>
<BODY>
<H1>My First Web Page</H1>
<P>This is my first web page.<BR>
It shows how easy HTML is.</P>
</BODY>
</HTML>
```

This page is very simple and lacks one of the most important features of a web page – a hyperlink. A hyperlink can point to a number of different sources of information, including another web page, an E-mail address, or a word-processor document.

Step 2: adding hyperlinks

The <A HREF=". . ."> tag is used to denote a hyperlink, with the reference to the other information source contained within the inverted commas. The </A> tag is used to end a hyperlink. Some examples of hyperlinks are shown below:

- <A HREF="second.htm"> – a link to a second web page stored in the same place.

- <A HREF="http://www.bmj.com"> – A link to the BMJ's web site

- <A HREF="mailto:someone@somewhere.com"> – Sends an e-mail to someone's e-mail account.

- <A HREF="./documents/example.doc"> – Allows you to download a document called example.doc from the documents sub-directory.

To add these hyperlinks to our web page as a bulleted list we can use the <UL> tag, which denotes an un-indexed list. The <IL> tag is used for an indexed list and would number each point from 1 to 4. To indicate the start of each item within the list, the <LI> tag is used. The page would look like Figure 11. 2, produced by the following HTML code:

```
<HTML>
<HEAD>
<TITLE>My First Web Page</TITLE>
</HEAD>
<BODY>
```

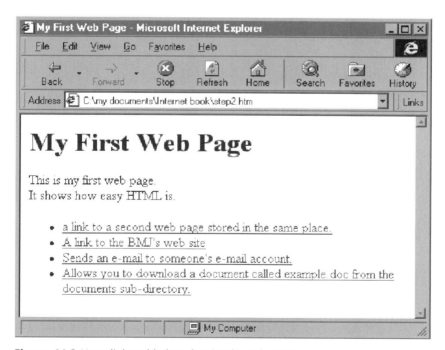

Figure 11.2 Hyperlinks added to the simple web page.

```
<H1>My First Web Page</H1>
<P>This is my first web page.<BR>
It shows how easy HTML is.</P>
<UL>
<LI><A HREF="second.htm">
a link to a second web page stored in the same place.
</A></LI>
<LI><A HREF="http://www.bmj.com">
A link to the BMJ's web site
</A></LI>
<LI><A HREF="mailto:someone@somewhere.com">
Sends an e-mail to someone's e-mail account.
</A></LI>
<LI><A HREF="./documents/example.doc">
Allows you to download a document called example.doc from
the documents sub-directory.
</A></LI>
</UL>
</BODY>
</HTML>
```

You now have a web page that links to two other web pages, a document for downloading, and to an E-mail address. This is a simple and effective web page; however, this simplicity could be translated as uninteresting. To make the page more appealing it is possible to add graphics.

Step 3: adding a graphic

To add an image to the example web page, you use the <IMG> tag. If your image is saved as example.gif in the same directory as the web page, the tag would be <IMG SRC="example.gif"> as the HTML tag needs to indicate where the image source is stored. As the details regarding the image are stored within the <IMG> tag, it is not necessary to have a </IMG> tag.

Another useful graphic device is horizontal line as it helps to separate different sections of text from one another. To add a horizontal line or 'rule', you need to insert a <HR> tag.

If you added a horizontal rule underneath the example web pages header and added a graphic called example.gif into the page before

Figure 11.3 Adding graphics to the web page.

the list of hyperlinks, as in the following HTML code, the page would appear as Figure 11.3.

```
<HTML>
<HEAD>
<TITLE>My First Web Page</TITLE>
</HEAD>
<BODY>
<H1>My First Web Page</H1>
<HR>
<P>This is my first web page.<BR>
It shows how easy HTML is.</P>
<IMG SRC="example.gif">
```

```
<UL>
<LI><A HREF="second.htm">
a link to a second web page stored in the same place.
</A></LI>
<LI><A HREF="http://www.bmj.com">
A link to the BMJ's web site
</A></LI>
<LI><A HREF="mailto:someone@somewhere.com">
Sends an e-mail to someone's e-mail account.
</A></LI>
<LI><A HREF="./documents/example.doc">
Allows you to download a document called example.doc from the
documents sub-directory.
</A></LI>
</UL>
</BODY>
</HTML>
```

Graphics explained: GIF and JPEG

Perhaps the most common component added to web pages is an image. These vary from photographs to clip-art to graphic text. Images of text are also used to overcome the limits of HTML's text formatting capabilities. Most web page designers use one of two image manipulation software packages to produce their images. The two packages are: PaintShop Pro, which is freely available from the Internet for a limited period of evaluation, and Adobe Photoshop, which is the choice of professional photographers and graphic designers but also has a high price. A wide range of other graphics packages and image manipulation utilities are available.

To add a graphic to a web page, you first need to save the image in one of the two formats commonly found on the web, which most browsers can easily read. These two formats are called GIF and JPEG. The choice of format will depend on the image, with the GIF format used for computer graphics and images that contain blocks of colour. The JPEG format was designed originally for photographs, and this means that this format is more suitable for complex, multicoloured images or photographs. If you are unsure which format is best suited to a particular image, the easiest solution is to save the image in both formats and then check which is the smaller file.

For this example page, if you do not have an image in GIF or JPEG format, or if you do not possess the software to save an image in one of these formats, you can copy an image from any site on the Internet. To copy an image, right-click the mouse on the image on the relevant web page and select the 'Save image as . . .' option. This allows you to copy the image to your own computer's hard disk. If you want to copy a picture or graphic from a web site, you should ensure that you are not breaching the copyright of the image.

Colours – and screen resolutions

As computer software has progressed from text-only displays to graphics, like Microsoft Windows, the computer hardware has also had to improve. This means that the computers used to access the Internet vary widely in the quality of their display. The importance of this to web page designers is that they must design their pages to display correctly on not only their own computer screen, but also on the wide variety of screens used by the page's target audience. Therefore, some understanding of computer display technology is required to ensure that pages are displayed correctly.

The quality of a computer's display is measured in two ways, the resolution of the image and the number of colours available to build this image. The resolution is measured by the number of pixels which make up the complete display. A pixel is the smallest, controllable area of a computer screen. Each pixel is a small dot that can change colour, and combine with the surrounding pixels to create a picture, in the same manner as a pointillist painting. The basic display resolution of most PCs is 640 pixels by 480 pixels, referred to as 640×480 or as VGA. Most PCs sold today are capable of much higher resolutions than this, with resolutions of 800×600, 1024×768, and higher available. The higher the resolution, the better the image quality as the pixels will be smaller and images on the screen appear smoother-edged or less 'pixellated'. Higher resolutions also mean that the amount of information displayed will increase, as there is a greater area to the display. The quality of the display also depends on the number of colours used to compose the image. The basic numbers of colours used for a VGA display is 256 colours, with $16\,000$, $24\,000$, and $32\,000$ available on modern PCs.

When designing a web site, it is important to consider the display quality of your potential audience. On the World Wide Web, with its wide audience, the probable minimum display quality will be 640×480 and 256 colours. This will ensure that nearly all visitors will see the site as intended, except for the small minority of web users still using text-based browsers. To meet the demands of every user involves ensuring that there is also a version of your site without graphics.

This resolution imposes limitations on the layout and amount of information displayed on screen. This has resulted in some sites being designed for displays with a minimum of 800×600 and $16\,000$ colours, as most PCs sold in the past few years are capable of displaying at this resolution.

Designing for the Web

The Web provides a new way of providing and sharing information with other organisations and individuals outside your organisation, or even within an organisation via an Intranet. However, as with any new means of communication, great care must be taken when transferring information from an existing source, such as a brochure or handbook, into a web page. Unfortunately, what looks good on A4 paper rarely looks good on the computer screen when viewed through a web browser.

The web is used to transfer information between computers, and to display this information on a computer screen. The physical size of a monitor and the amount of information it can display at one time enforce limitations on the design of web pages. Also the average web user will move quickly to the next web site if he or she encounters a long textual web page, as it is more tiring to read a long monologue from a computer screen than from a paper-based medium.

This means that web pages should bear more resemblance to magazines and brochures than to books and reports, with short passages of text interspersed with images or links to other pages. It also means that great care should be taken when converting a paper-based document into a web page, as what looks good on a sheet of A4 paper rarely looks as appealing on a computer screen.

The other major concern when designing for the web is the time it will take the reader to download the full page from the Internet. As with the screen resolution problems discussed earlier, the best practice is to design the page with consideration for the user of a low-specification connection. For download speeds, a typical low specification would be an Internet user with a modem rated at 28.8 Kbps. For an Intranet site, the download speed will probably be higher as most users will have a direct connection. However, with regard to the NHSWeb, the spread of the Intranet to GP surgeries means that more users will be using modem connections.

Web page-designers can easily add too many components to their web sites, or make the presentation over complex. A common source of frustration for the web user is waiting patiently for a large graphic to appear on screen to discover that the image bears little relation to the other content on screen, or provides no additional benefit.

The web page designer has also a much freer reign in relation to the colours and textures used in a site. As there are no constraints imposed by the printing process, it is possible to use a wide range of colours and images to enhance a site. This is made even easier by the wide variety of images available via the web, designed especially for display on the web. This not only includes clip-art images and photographs, but also animated cartoons and textures and backdrops designed especially for use as a background. This allows the web designer to produce pages with multicoloured backgrounds, or textured backdrops such as wood or marble. These can be used with a wide variety of images and text in a myriad of colours. However, this freedom of design also makes it much easier to produce ill-matched combinations which reduce legibility and hinder the reading of the page's content.

What constitutes 'good' design is a subject that raises much debate among the Internet community, with sites devoted to what makes a well-designed site, and other sites devoted to what makes a badly designed site. Before building a web site it is advisable to visit some of these sites and also to decipher the reasons why some sites look good to you, and why others do not appeal.

More advanced HTML & design

HTML was originally conceived as medium for sharing information between scientists, where the emphasis was on structuring the data rather than producing eye-catching designs. As the Web has matured, web page authoring has incorporated many aspects of design from other media, and it has also developed its own techniques that are particularly suited to the Web. These aim to produce better-designed sites, which make it easier for visitors to find the information that they seek.

One of the most common design elements incorporated into web pages is the use of a table to lay out the information across the breadth of the screen. By using tables without a border around the table cells, a designer can produce a site reminiscent of a newspaper layout, with the information spread over a number of columns. The <TABLE> tag marks the beginning of a table, with the <TR> tag denoting the start of a row and <TD> indicating a cell within the row.

A page constructed using tables is still very simple, bearing a resemblance to a sheet of paper displayed on screen. It is possible to split the screen into a number of separate pages, with the ability to control the content of one screen based on links contained within another screen, by using frames. A common use of frames is to split the screen into two sections, with one section containing a list of available pages and the second showing the relevant page.

The Web also offers the designer the ability to add multimedia facilities to their web site, moving the Web further away from its text-based heritage.

One of the most common types of multimedia components are small animations based upon GIF images. These animated GIFs consist of a number of images, much like individual still images in a roll of film. They can be constructed quite easily using software packages like the GIF construction kit, which can be downloaded easily from a number of sites on the Web. These animated GIFs can add movement to a site or bring attention to certain parts of a site. A good example of an animated GIF is the posting of a letter in a post-box, to highlight an E-mail address (of which there are several freely available versions).

Java

The features discussed within this chapter are built into the HTML language; however, there is another programming language which has made a widespread impact on the Web, called Java. Java is a modern programming language, compared to the relatively basic scripting allowed by HTML. This means that the programmer can make certain 'events' happen in response to the actions of the visitor to the site. These actions can vary from complex calculations to giving the impression of a button being pushed when the visitor clicks the mouse on it.

As Java is a fully fledged programming language, it is not as simple for the novice user to learn as HTML. However, several software packages are available that hide the complexity of Java programming behind a user-friendly interface. This makes simple Java programs, called 'applets', available to most web page designers. However, although Java is a widely recognised standard, older browsers are incapable of understanding Java applets and this is one of the main reasons that the initial promises have not materialised.

Although Java has made an impact on the Internet, but to a lesser extent than initially forecast, an offshoot called JavaScript has gained a much wider audience. This language bears more resemblance to HTML but gives the designer some of the freedom offered by Java. It is used by a large number of sites to add interactivity and multimedia elements to their web pages.

In relation to forms, JavaScript is often used to validate the content of a form. It can be used to ensure that information has been entered in all the compulsory fields, e.g. name or E-mail address, or to check that the information entered matches one of the valid values for that field. As the JavaScript is contained within the web page that has been downloaded, this is undertaken by the visitor's own computer. This is called client-side processing. The advantages of client-side processing include faster responses, due to the calculations being undertaken on the visitor's computer, and a reduction in the workload of the web server.

Forms and CGI

This chapter has dealt with putting information onto a web site, but it is also possible to gain information from your site. This can be done by asking visitors to complete feedback forms or question-naires.

To add a form to a web page you need to use the form tags <FORM> and </FORM> to denote the start and end of the form. There are also a number of types of field which can be used within a form, including a text box and option buttons.

Once the visitor has completed the form the information needs to be either stored or sent to its destination. To achieve this, the content of the form has to be processed by the computer that stores the web page – the web server. Unfortunately, the HTML language does not have the capabilities to process this information, so the processing must be handled by a separate program. The standard programs used to perform the processing use CGI (common gateway interface), and the program files are stored in a separate directory called CGI-BIN. The programs can be written in a number of languages (the most popular is PERL) but there are also a large number of sample programs for the most common tasks, such as feedback forms and visitor comment forms, freely available from a number of sources on the Web.

Posting pages

Once you have created your web site, you need to get the pages onto the Internet. There are several ways of establishing a presence on the Internet, but the core requirement is access to a web server. One of the most popular methods for individuals and small organ-isations is to use the 'free' web space provided by ISPs as part of their Internet access packages. This is a very cheap and easy solution as there is no additional charge over and above the monthly connection fee. Also, most ISPs offer facilities designed for the novice web page designer, such as free CGI programs for processing forms, and hit counters for counting the number of visitors to the site. The disadvantages of this approach include relatively slow connection speeds, a limited amount of space on the server and long URLs, which look less professional because they include details of the ISP in the name (e.g. *www.someone.demon.co.uk*).

If you require more space than this, or want to register your own domain name, there are a number of commercial Internet service providers, or commercial divisions of the consumer-orientated ISPs. These offer larger spaces on their web servers, with faster connec-tions, and are discussed further in Chapter 8.

For large organisations the next logical step is to purchase their own web server with a permanent, direct connection to the Internet. This is a very expensive option, as not only will you need to purchase high-powered computer equipment, but you will also need technically qualified staff to maintain it.

On the Intranet, the situation is reversed – the most viable solution for most organisations is to organise their own web server.

Most health authorities and NHS Trusts will already have the necessary computer and network equipment installed, with the requisite staff to maintain them. The cost of connecting these existing networks into the networks of other organisations that form the NHSNet is very low in comparison to connecting to the Internet. One of the primary goals of an Intranet is to allow the dissemination of information from a variety of sources, and this means that most connected organisations actively encourage individuals and departments to contribute to the organisation's web site. This means that it is quite easy to gain space on one of these servers.

12 The future of the Internet

Introduction

There is probably as much written about the future developments of the Internet as there is about the current state of the system. The main reason for this is that the Internet has only recently become a mass communications medium, moving away from its technical background into a new media channel for the general public.

The Internet and, in particular, the Web are still immature consumer products with new potential markets frequently appearing and 'the next big thing' in Internet technology regularly failing to meet expectations. This gives the pundits a broad base for their assumptions and projections, whether optimistic or pessimistic, about the future of the Internet.

This chapter will look at some of the technologies currently under development that will extend the potential of the Internet and overcome some of its shortcomings. It will also look at how these developments and others may affect the use of the Internet and Intranets in the future, with particular emphasis on how these will affect the NHS, patients, and healthcare professionals.

Developments

The further development of the Internet and the expanding user base present new technical problems for the administrators. The uncontrolled growth of the Internet and the expansion of the system beyond the wildest dreams of the original instigators present two major problems. These are increasing the speed of access and providing enough unique IP addresses for all these new users.

The IP address system is based on providing each user with a unique IP address, consisting of four numbers between 0 and 255, for example 244.12.98.143. This is sufficient for over 4 billion addresses, which was felt to provide sufficient for any expansion of the system by the original designers of the IP protocol. Further refinement of the system, using a subcode called a sub-net mask, has allowed this number to be increased even further. Unfortunately this is still not enough numbers for the burgeoning Internet community.

Although there are more addresses than users, some people have more than one address and, to ease administration, countries and large organisations are allocated blocks of numbers; for example, an organisation may be provided with 244.12.98.0 to 244.12.98.255. This means that it is impossible to allocate each individual address to one person, effectively reducing the number of possible addresses.

The IP protocol has been improved a number of times, and it is currently on version 6; however, the development of the latest version of IP, called IPng (short for Internet protocol next generation), is designed to overcome these shortcomings and provide even more addresses.

To increase the speed of the Internet is a complex task that can be split into two separate areas: the backbone of the system that carries and routes the requests of millions of users at any given time, and increasing the speed of connection between each individual user and his or her ISP.

To improve the performance of the Internet's backbone involves a massive investment in computer networking research to find new ways of moving information through the infrastructure at even higher speeds. The US is leading this research and has a number of advanced projects currently under way within the academic and research community to test and develop these new techniques. The principal projects are the Internet2 project,[1] a collaboration of 1209 US universities, and the Next Generation Internet (NGI).[2] The NGI project is a government-run project that involves many government organisations including the Department of Defense's Advanced Research Projects Agency (the principal developer of the ARPANET which was the foundation of the Internet), NASA, and National Institutes of Health, among others. These projects are both designed to provide high-speed links, based upon the Internet protocols, between the organisations involved; however, the technology involved will probably become the backbone of the Internet in the future.

To increase the speed of the average user's connection also involves the development of alternative methods and means of communication. The latest standard of modems (V.90) can communicate at up to 56.6 Kbps, which is near the limit of telephone-line capabilities. This is demonstrated by the fact that these modems cannot transmit at more than 33.6 Kbps, due to limitations in the quality of domestic telephone lines and exchanges, whereas they can receive at 56.6 Kbps due to the higher-quality telephone-line links implemented by ISPs.

Because of the massive costs involved in re-cabling consumer's homes with higher-quality lines, alternative delivery methods are required. The simplest improvement is the use of an ISDN line, which provides a digital telephone line and is currently capable of speeds of up to 128 Kbps. This is very simple as most of the work is undertaken at the telephone exchange to convert an existing phone line from analogue to digital, with only a change in the type of connection being necessary in the home. You will also need an ISDN modem, referred to as a terminal adaptor (TA).

An emerging telephone technology is ADSL (asynchronous digital subscriber line) that promises speeds of up to 1.5 Mbps (i.e. 1500 Kbps) and is beginning to be implemented by British Telecom. It is not currently recognised by the International Telecommunication Union (ITU), which ratifies all international telecommunication standards, but once it is approved it should offer very high speeds at relatively low cost. Once it becomes widespread and the cost of installation drops to a level suitable for home use, it should be possible to have video-quality images over the Internet, and other high-definition services will be within reach of the general public.

Other solutions could involve the utilisation of the other cabling infrastructure that is common in consumer's homes and small offices. Perhaps the most innovative are the plans to provide Internet connections via the national grid, which is being developed by some electricity companies. The Internet transmissions are routed through the existing electricity cabling. The other major option that can be developed to meet its potential is the cable network operated by the cable TV organisations. This utilises fibre optic cables and could provide Internet connections at much higher speeds than that obtainable through ISDN. However, the cable operators have so far been slow to exploit this market, with only a few cable modems becoming available.

All these technologies are being designed to provide faster and easier connections to the Internet, overcoming the shortcomings of the existing infrastructure and making Internet access transparent to the user. However, perhaps the greatest change in the future will be how and where the user accesses the Internet.

Currently, any user of the Internet needs to be fairly computer literate and needs access to a computer before they can gain access to the Internet. In the future computers will still be one of the main methods of accessing the Internet, especially amongst business users. More people will also have computers at home, with the current trend for home usage of personal computers, or PC compatible computers, continuing to grow. However, there will also be newer, cheaper computers, designed primarily for accessing the Internet and deriving most of their software and features from the Internet. This simplified computing power will reduce the cost of the equipment, making these computers accessible to a larger proportion of the population.

But Internet access will not be restricted to computer users, with the Internet accessible through domestic TV or on a display attached to a telephone. Web TV is already available, and could become the primary means of consumer Internet access. Other devices will also offer Internet access, such as telephones with built-in web browsers. This type of access can already be seen in some mobile phones and personal digital assistants (PDAs) like the Psion range.

E-commerce

The roots of the Internet in the academic and research community are quite apparent in its structure and the open forum for ideas that it provides. Although this openness and lack of censure has been one of the driving forces behind its development and its appeal, this lack of control makes it very difficult to run commercial operations via the Internet.

Businesses require rules and regulations to preserve their intellectual rights and to allow them to profit from their products. Therefore for E-commerce to succeed, the Internet community needs to find a balance between its freedom and the control needed for commerce. The key elements required by businesses are adequate security to allow consumers to feel confident in purchasing via the Web, and a method of ensuring that they retain copyright upon their intellectual property.

The level of security required to provide secure transactions across the Internet is more a question of gaining consumer confidence rather than ensuring that no unauthorised use is made of credit-card details. Although very few consumers currently have enough confidence in the Internet to provide their credit-card details via the Web, it is likely that these same people will disclose their details to other unknown people. For example, over the telephone to a sales person of a mail order company or handing over their credit card to a waiter in a restaurant. Some notable exponents of web-based sales, such as Dell computers and Amazon bookstore, have provided secure web-based credit-card transactions for some time.

However, to provide confidence in the security of Internet transactions a new standard has been devised, called SET (secure electronic transaction). This promises to provide the requisite security to ensure that your credit-card details, etc. can only be read by the authorised recipient and can not be intercepted. The SET standard is currently gaining acceptance and should become the *de facto* standard in the next few years.

The protection of intellectual rights and preservation of trade-marks is a more difficult issue to resolve. The inherent weaknesses in the security of the Internet mean that it is quite easy, and indeed is common practice, for web users to steal parts of sites. This can be due to a number of reasons, not all malicious, as it is common practice for web page designers to copy parts of other designers' sites where the design appeals to them. If the copied parts are the furniture of the site, i.e. buttons or background colours, then there is unlikely to be an issue of copyright. However, if someone copies the content of a web page and passes this as their work, there is an obvious breach of copyright. The pursuit of a copyright claim is very difficult due to the cross-border nature of the Internet, as it could involve a lengthy and costly international court case. For this reason the Internet will probably not become the prevalent source of new material and texts where copyright is a dominant issue.

The preservation of trademarks and company names is another difficult area, but this issue is being resolved. There has been some conflict between the need of businesses to preserve their name and identity and the loosely regulated domain name registration bodies. This has led to some opportunists registering well-known trade names and then trying to sell them to the organisations who trade under these names, at an inflated cost. The high courts have ruled in favour of the trade-name holders in a case against one such opportunist company called 'one in a million' and this will hopefully discourage other profiteers. The Internet community is also begin-ning to realise that as the commercial aspects of the Internet expand some compromises in the structure need to be made to allow these commercial organisations to trade over the Internet.

By addressing these issues, the Internet and, in particular, the Web should see explosive growth in the number of organisations trading electronically. The benefits of trading over the Web make this an attractive method of selling products and services. These benefits include low overhead costs, as all that is needed is a web server and permanent Internet connection that provides service for 24 hours a day, 7 days a week. This compares to the large sales force and retail outlets required by more traditional sales methods. An on-line catalogue of products will also cost a fraction of the traditional paper-based version, and can also be easily updated. The benefits of these lower overheads to the consumer vary, but most E-commerce sites offer some inducement to purchase on-line, either by lower prices or by improved specifications at the same cost. As the E-commerce market is global rather than regional, the level of competition is much higher and the potential market much larger, therefore making the market place much more competitive and price sensitive. Due to this, the savings obtained by shopping on line are likely to increase as more companies compete.

The future implications for the NHS

The Internet and Intranet are seen as providing a key communication medium for the NHS. The government has put the development of the Intranet at the forefront of the modernisation of the NHS, with a number of stated commitments regarding E-mail and the type of information that will be available via the Intranet.

With all GPs, Trusts, and health authorities having E-mail, the communication of health information will be faster and cheaper than traditional methods. One study conducted in America in the early 1990s estimated that the US health system could save $30 billion a year with improved use of telecommunications.[3] The use of the Intranet and Internet to realise these savings is dependent on the successful adoption of E-mail and the NHSWeb as primary sources of information exchange.

If they are widely adopted, it will allow the development of a wide variety of services, such as on-line booking of outpatient appointments by GPs, reduced waiting times for test results, and easier access to the latest medical information. It could also provide the means of accessing and storing the electronic health record (EHR) as outlined in the NHS Executive's *Information for Health* report.[4]

With the help of new web-access devices like hand-held personal digital assistants (PDAs), etc. and improving mobile telecommunications, this information will not only be available to the GP in his or her clinic room, or the nursing staff on a hospital ward. The GP on house calls and the primary healthcare team working in the community will be able to use this information. This mobility of data has been possible for some time, but it has relied on expensive proprietary technology. The Internet and Web provide a generic and inexpensive means of transmitting and viewing information, bringing the technology into the mainstream.

Due to the increasing demand for E-commerce, transactions across the Internet will become safer and faster. For healthcare, this will help resolve the issues concerning the secure transmission of confidential patient data across the Internet. This is perhaps the greatest obstacle in the widespread adoption of the Internet as a viable means of communication. The future should allow healthcare professionals to be confident that any information sent or received via the Internet will retain its security and confidentiality.

The future implications for patients

The Internet allows patients access to the latest information about a wide variety of medical conditions. This is already leading to some individuals self-diagnosing their conditions based upon the information they have gathered from their web searches. From the medical practitioner's perspective this will offer both benefits and problems, with better-informed patients recognising problems or symptoms earlier and therefore improving the chances of successful treatment. The other side to this is the greater potential for misinformation, due not only to the larger volume of material available, but also from the amount of poor information available. One study showed that the advice given for treating a feverish child could be misleading, with some sites advising the use of aspirin that would put the child at risk of Reye's syndrome.[5] Also with increased knowledge, patients will begin to question the chosen treatment or diagnoses, resulting in medical practitioners needing to justify their decisions more fully. Therefore the NHS has to provide high-quality information via the Web, enabling patients to visit a site that they can be confident provides the best current information about a wide range of medical conditions and health-related issues. This

141

information service should form part of the 'NHS Direct' initiative that is using more traditional means, such as telephone helplines, to provide this type of information.

Another possibility is that the traditional route of diagnosis from GP to hospital may be usurped, with patients bypassing the NHS and using their credit card to purchase healthcare via the Web. It could be possible for a patient to send images, taken with a digital camera, to a specialist in Australia, through an Internet-enabled TV, for diagnoses.

The future implications for health professionals

The Internet and Intranet should become the prime source of reference material for most healthcare professionals. They will allow the medical practitioner easy access to the latest information and advice regarding most medical conditions. The widespread availability of high-quality information will also aid research into best practice, and therefore raise the quality of healthcare. Distance learning will also provide wider opportunities, allowing medical practitioners and researchers to learn from the world's leading experts.

The Intranet will provide the latest information within the NHS, but the Internet offers much greater opportunities, by allowing the world's top specialists to disseminate information on a global scale. It will also become possible for these specialists to be consulted from anywhere in the world via multimedia links. This means that a patient in the UK could seek second opinions from specialists in the US, Italy, etc. It will be even more significant in the developing world, where the expertise of the world's best could be made available for routine clinics or in times of disaster or conflict.[6] Therefore, the Internet provides a means of accessing better-quality information anywhere in the world, aiding medical diagnosis and allowing better treatment-plan management on a global scale. This should help improve the health of the world population through the hands of better-informed clinical practitioners.

References

1 www.internet2.edu
2 www.ngi.gov

3   Little AD (1992) *Telecommunications: Can it Help Solve America's Health Care problems?* Arthur D Little, Cambridge, MA.

4   Burns F (1998) *Information for Health.* NHS Executive, Leeds.

5   Impicciatore P, Pandolfini C, Casella N, *et al.* (1997) Reliability of information for the public on the World Wide Web: systematic advice on managing fever in children at home. *BMJ* **314**: 1875.

6   Rogers R (1998) *Br J Hlthcare Comput Inform Manag* **15**(5), 30-32.

Index